SMALLMOUTH BASS FISHING

FOR EVERYONE

SMALLMOUTH BASS FISHING

FOR EVERYONE

How to Catch the Hardest Fighting Fish That Swims

JAMES ROOT

Skyhorse Publishing

For my dad.
It made all the difference.

Skyhorse Publishing books may be purchased in bulk at special discounts for sales promotion, corporate gifts, fund-raising, or educational purposes. Special editions can also be created to specifications. For details, contact the Special Sales Department, Skyhorse Publishing, 307 West 36th Street, 11th Floor, New York, NY 10018 or info@skyhorsepublishing.com.

Skyhorse® and Skyhorse Publishing® are registered trademarks of Skyhorse Publishing, Inc.®, a Delaware corporation.

Visit our website at www.skyhorsepublishing.com.

10 9 8 7 6 5 4 3 2

Library of Congress Cataloging-in-Publication Data is available on file.

Cover design by Tom Lau
Cover photo credit: Jon Fuchs

ISBN: 978-1-5107-1590-5
Ebook ISBN: 978-1-5107-1592-9

Printed in China

Contents

Foreword

Mark Zona and his two sons.

My entire life has been spent chasing almost every freshwater species of fish. I have fished the oceans and caught sharks and fish that weigh thousands of pounds. I've chased nearly all of them and the point is, ultimately, smallmouth bass are my number one species. When it comes to my thoughts on smallmouth bass fishing, I tell people this: "My career is fishing, my passion is smallmouth bass." On a beautiful fall day when you'd think, *gosh, today is just a perfect day to hunt,* my mind will be on one of my smallmouth spots and wondering what they're biting on today.

I've been all over the world and I've learned one really important thing about small-mouth bass and the men and women who chase them: We are our own subculture. Other fish come and go, but to us smallmouth fishing is always where we wanna be. We speak a language entirely our own, and we know instantly when we meet another person who's been bitten by smallmouth fever. I knew that about Jim the first time I spoke to him. In fact, one of the first times we spoke to each other I think I told him, "I know you're a smallmouth psycho like me!" Smallmouth addicts understand that it's a commitment of lifelong learning, that you think you know smallmouth but then something happens and you're reminded that you don't!

The people you're going to read about in this book—KVD, Mangus, Noffsigner, Palaniuk, Zaldain, Tony DeFilippo, Steve Clapper, George Acordi Jr.—have spent years learning about smallmouth. They have cut their teeth trying to solve the riddle. Some of them are the same people that taught me. The places in this book, the lakes and rivers from Mille Lacs, to Traverse City, to The Great Lakes and The Susquehanna River, these are the places where I go to film my shows because they're the Lambeau Fields, the Fenway Parks, The Coliseums; they're the greatest stadiums for the ultimate fish. If you're intrigued by smallmouth and the obsession, this book is for you.

—Mark Zona

Introduction

My name is Jim Root, and two years ago I took a break from Tournament Fishing on the Bassmaster circuit to focus on one thing: finding the biggest smallmouth bass in the world. That mission has pushed me from the most prestigious waters to the most remote, in search of the biggest, meanest, and heaviest smallmouth in existence. From Tennessee to Texas to the Northernmost reaches of Ontario, Canada, to find the smallmouth of a lifetime and the brothers and sisters they are swimming with. Smallmouth are pack animals. They're incredibly aggressive feeders and are regarded as some of the fiercest fighting fish pound for pound. Locating them is the hardest part. Find them, and they'll eat.

Where to find big smallmouth depends on where you're fishing and what the conditions are during different periods of the year. They are incredibly nomadic creatures, with studies that have shown their ability to travel over thirty-five miles in just one day. This much movement can make finding fish day after day difficult, particularly in rivers. But the migratory habits are essentially broken down into two areas—deep and shallow—that make finding them a bit easier. You have to keep in mind the relativity of each body of water. In a place

Sunrise. Shane Durrance

like the Mississippi, shallow can mean something very different than it does in a place like the Susquehanna. So for our purposes we're going to say that shallow is under ten feet, and deep is over ten feet. In the spring, when the water warms above 50°F, the smallmouth will move to shallow water. They'll be looking for any creeks that enter the river, as these are some of their favorite places to spawn.

After spawning and as summer approaches, the fish will retreat to deeper water where they'll tend to spend most of their time during the summer months as long as the water is clean and has good current. In the fall they'll move shallow again and begin feeding ferociously. This can be one of the most exciting times to fish for any species. How long this feeding frenzy will last depends entirely on Mother Nature. If winter holds off, and the temperatures hover in that 40°F–55°F range, the season can last well into December. If winter comes earlier and the water cools off, then the bite will be exciting but the fish will move back to deep water to their wintering holes. These holes may or may not be the same places where they summer, depending on many other characteristics on that body of water. For instance, on the Susquehanna there are warm water discharges that might be of very little appeal to smallmouth in the summer, but can be heavily loaded with fish in cold weather for many reasons that I'll discuss later on. But you see the cyclical pattern here: deep, to shallow, to deep, to shallow.

In lakes, however, this can be a little different. While the fish still tend to winter in deeper holes and move shallow in the spring for feeding and prespawn activities, they'll often lay their eggs much deeper (I've seen smallmouth beds in 25 feet), and won't always return to those deeper holes in the summer. Oneida Lake is a prime example of this. Some of my favorite places to fish at Oneida in the summer are in areas that hold both smallmouth and largemouth bass together. These areas are between 7–12 feet deep, but I've caught big smallmouth at Oneida in July in water as shallow as just a few inches on a rocky shoreline. For this reason, in my opinion, smallmouth bass that live in lakes can be much more difficult to pinpoint from day to day, especially when you're trying to follow a big school of fish. This nomadic characteristic is what makes smallmouth bass hard to catch.

My knowledge of smallmouth bass has come from an equal mix of time on the water, and studying and learning as much as I could from people who knew them better than me. I remember during my first year on the tournament trail I was fishing as a co-angler and I was doing pretty well. I think at the halfway point of the year I was in the top five for angler of the year points standings and we were going into one of the last events at Cayuga Lake, which I considered to be my home lake at the time, after having just lived on the east shore of that lake in Aurora for two years. I was paired with Larry Mazur, and I didn't realize at the time, but he's one of the best deepwater anglers in the world. We talked a little bit before and I told him that I knew that lake very well and that we could catch a lot of fish really shallow (less than five feet). He looked at me and said "The only time you'll ever see my boat in less

Chenango River smallmouth.

than five feet of water is if I'm sinking!" Come tournament time I melted down, could not wrap my head around fishing deep, and I zeroed. Which sent me from third in points, to like fifteenth, and although I was able to rebound and finish the season in the top ten, the points championship was not at all possible. This taught me a very valuable lesson. Watching Larry work deep water was incredible. I even drew him again in the same year, at Oneida, and I saw how he targeted the smallmouth there and I watched him all day. He also showed me what it was like to be a professional, to help teach, share baits and knowledge to grow the sport. We still fish together, I still learn from him, and I've been able to share some things with him too. You'll see some incredible pictures of him and me later on in this book.

I've been fortunate enough to meet other deepwater experts like Brandon Palaniuk, who I fish with at least once a year on various smallmouth waters in New York. Like Larry, Brandon is really great about sharing what he's learned. If you get an opportunity to spend time with these people on the water, don't waste it. Ask questions about their use of electronics, what they're looking for, why they're searching in particular areas, and why they're using certain baits. People say I share too much information. This book will probably be the exclamation point at the end of that statement. It should be noted, though, that going after the biggest smallmouth in North America means having to fish some of the biggest bodies

Lake Ontario.

of water, and with that comes a fair amount of risk and I can't stress the severity of that enough. Being properly prepared and taking necessary precautions is significant enough that I dedicated an entire chapter to it in this book. Of all the pages herein those are the ones that every reader should pay very close attention to. Every year in Upstate New York we read about people who made one small mistake that cost them their life, and there are a million different ways that this can happen.

This book is a testament to what you can do if you believe in yourself. I grew up dirt poor. Some nights in the winter my brother and I walked two miles in the snow with bottles and cans and empty gas cans so that we could get a couple dollars of kerosene to run our furnace. I could fill these pages with the number of rejection letters I've gotten along the way, but I never gave up. Wealth is not the only path to opportunity. Believe in yourself, and work hard, and you can have anything you want. Lastly, I want you, the reader, to know that I poured everything I have into this book, that I held nothing back. There's not one ounce of smallmouth secrecy left within me after completing this, and I know that if you read it, it will help you catch the biggest smallmouth of your life.

PART I

The Smallmouth Bass: Its Life Cycle, Seasons, Habits, and Recommended Equipment for Catching It

1

What Are Smallmouth?

What are smallmouth bass? Smallmouth bass (*Micropterus dolomieu*) are my greatest passion. The largest ever recorded was 27 inches long and weighed over 12 pounds. An average male weighs 2 pounds, and females weigh an average of 3–6 pounds and can carry as much as twenty-one thousand eggs that are guarded by males during the spawn in the spring. When people ask me "What are smallmouth?" I tend to give them the technical answer:

A smallmouth bass is a freshwater fish that is predominantly found north of the Mason-Dixon line. Smallmouth prefer cold, moving water, and are the primary game fish in the Great Lakes because they're known for their acrobatic ability to jump out of the water, and for their tremendous fighting ability.

While I'm giving that answer, what I'm really thinking is:

Smallies are the most badass freshwater fish you'll ever catch. People who've caught them will call them smallies, bronzebacks, small jaws, small dawgs, brownies, and brown fish. I actually think the most beautiful ones are that crystal green color, not the black or brown. I can't wait to get back to Ontario again and . . .

Then I refocus, talk about how hard they fight, and why I'm so addicted to catching them. Catching smallmouth is really not hard. It's hard to find a more aggressive freshwater fish. If you can find smallmouth, most of the time you can get them to eat fairly easily. But finding them is the key. Brandon Palaniuk described them best when he said "They're so nomadic by nature that it's like they can't stay in one place for too long." He's absolutely right. You can find a huge school of big smallmouth, know exactly what they want to eat, and how they want to eat it. You can hammer that school for an entire day. You can come

Lake Erie. Jon Fuchs

back the next day and see that they're still there and hammer them again, and again, and again. Or you can return the next day to see that they've vanished without a trace to track them down.

As a species there are things that set them apart more than others, for example, their affinity for cold water. Being cold-blooded, it would stand to reason that they'd want the warmest water they could find, but that is not the case. Because smallmouth dwell in deeper water, it can really be difficult for beginners to locate them. What's also interesting about smallmouth is that they have been known to carry their eggs for the entire winter. This explains why smallmouth will feast in January, when their cousins the largemouth will go into a winter feeding mode and eat only once a day, and typically small meals at that. Smallmouth are highly predatory. These fish do not eat plants, or pieces of bread. Smallmouth are carnivores. Make no mistake about that simply because they don't have teeth like you're used to seeing in tigers or lions, or even in fish like pike or musky. Smallmouth eat other living things, period.

As nomadic and elusive as smallmouth appear to be, there's a pattern to their madness. You can learn and exploit their habitual routine of migration and feeding. This knowledge won't ensure that you'll never have another bad day, but it will make them happen much less. I've spent close to twenty years chasing these brown fish. When I enter the town of Brownville near the eastern end of Lake Ontario my hair stands up on my arms and I feel lighter, just knowing how close I am to where something incredible could happen. I know their movements, what they prefer to eat, how to make them eat when they won't do it willingly, and most of all I'm confident beyond explanation and that is my greatest asset. I've caught so many trophy smallmouth in my life that I can usually predict when it'll happen. I can feel that the bait is moving right, that I'm on big fish, and that I'm going to hook one any minute. And now I'm giving all that knowledge to you. What I didn't learn from my own trial and error I learned from some of the greatest smallmouth fishermen in the world. Larry Mazur, Brandon Palaniuk, Chris Zaldain, Mark Zona, Bill Lortz, John McGoey, Jimmy Kennedy, and guys you've never heard of who have caught more 7-plus-pound smallmouth than most people have even seen, let alone touched.

Small mouth, but big attitude. The first big smallie you hook into that leaps three feet out of the water and shakes your hook will have you addicted forever.

2

Boat Prep

Taking proper care of your boat is really important, but when you're talking about going after giant smallmouth you want to be sure to take every added precaution available to you. Throughout the course of the next several chapters you're going to be reading about some incredibly beautiful places: The St. Lawrence River, The Great Lakes, The Susquehanna River, Sturgeon Bay, The New River, Oneida Lake, Lake Simcoe, Lake Champlain, and many others. While widely known for their beauty, they also have a reputation for rapidly changing weather conditions that can cause nautical conditions that require preparation. I really can't stress this enough to people who haven't seen it. The weather you could (and most likely will) encounter is more like the ocean than it is a lake or pond, and to try to shed light on just how severe it can get I want to tell you a story about perspective. My first time fishing in South Carolina, we were at the National Championship at Santee Cooper. It got a little windy that day, and my buddy Brian was paired up with a local guy who lived not far from Santee and fished it often. He was probably in his early twenties, and had been fishing quite a while, but at noon, nearly in tears, he begged Brian to bring him back to shore because the two-foot waves were too much. Those exact same conditions are what you will find on a normal day at many of the Great Lakes. In fact, you want to have that kind of wind because it turns the fish on like a light switch. To Brian, and many of us, that kind of wind and waves was completely normal, and not dangerous at all. But all things are viewed subjectively, and to Brian's co-angler, admittedly, he had never been in water that rough before. By comparison, I tell a lot of people a story of the first time I ever fished Lake Ontario and threw up four times because we had some waves that were close to 6 feet and at one point I was reeling in a fish while we were down in the trough of the wave that was eye level with me, and I could see it swimming in front of me.

I'm not trying to scare people out of going to these lakes. I choose to fish Ontario over any other lake because it's full of giants. But I don't want people to be unprepared, or to get there and be caught off guard and end up hurt. I also advise people who have never driven

A couple quick safety checks can save you lots of time later.

a bass boat in rough water to use caution and do a little research. In really rough water you can't drive easily by nosing head first into the wave. Sometimes you have to take a longer route by driving in the trough, kind of like needing to go from point A, to point C, to get to point B.

Fishing these lakes is some of the most heart-racing action you will ever find in fresh-water. But there are certain precautions that you need to take in order to be sure that your safety isn't jeopardized. To help you with this I've put together a fifteen-point checklist of items that every boater should inspect or install prior to navigating the rivers and/or lakes that are mentioned in this book. They cover everything from general maintenance, to fish care, to marine forecasts and more. So make note of these and be sure to check them before you go every time.

1. Bilge Pump
   This is the most important motorized part of your boat. If this goes, you're going to be in big trouble. And sometimes one isn't enough. Many people I know have multiple pumps installed on their boat. Not only will this save you if one quits, but if you do get caught in some really nasty weather you'll be glad you have a second.

2. Flare Gun, Fire Extinguisher

   These are really common sense things, but that flare gun will come in very handy on a lake that feels like the ocean when you're in the middle of it, or in a river valley that appears to be incredibly rural for as far as you can see.

3. Livewell Check

   It's really good to make sure your livewell works, but sometimes that's not enough. Small-mouth are incredibly delicate in the summer, and if you don't take proper care of them they'll die. Ice is not the best solution for livewells because it's made with water that's been treated by chlorine and other things that are not exactly "natural" to fish. Rejuvenade is a powder that people add to the livewell, and it's not a horrible solution, but it is pricey and doesn't last forever. Another option is a livewell system for your boat called the V-T2 made by New Pro Products. It circulates air through your livewell and increases oxygen levels. Another good idea is a bottle of citrus soda. If you do get a fish that is hooked poorly and starts bleeding you can pour a little in the area and it will cauterize the wound and stop it from bleeding. Who would've thought Sierra Mist could save a smallmouth's life.

4. Fizzing Tool

   This is absolutely key for smallmouth bass fishing, and you need to learn how to do it properly to keep your fish alive. Fizzing is taking a needle with an open end, and sticking it into the air bladder of the fish to relieve the air. First of all, let me say that if you're not keeping the fish in the livewell, you do not have to fizz them. You can take the hook off and put them right back in and they will dive back to the bottom. But if you plan to put them in the livewell for a tournament you have two choices: fizz them, or apply fin weights to keep them from floating upside down and dying (and the weights don't work). There are two ways to fizz fish: down their throat and through their side. Down the mouth is the way most people do it, but is also rumored to be the

Chris Zaldain fizzing an Ontario smallmouth.

more dangerous for the fish. The needle is sharp, and you don't want to be poking it around in their throat over and over again while you search for the right place. My good friend and fellow New York angler Barb Elliot has developed a map to help people learn how to do this. It's a really great tool and can be found online.

5. Lights
   This is probably the one thing that people seem most resistant to check. Having working lights can save your life. They draw a minimal amount of juice off the battery, and can be seen from miles away on clear nights.

6. Weather Radio
   My grampa gave me a windup light and weather radio for Christmas that actually works. Not only will it give me local weather, it will also charge my phone if I need it to. That could be huge.

7. Water
   If you do break down and have to overnight you need water. You can put a gallon of spring water in the boat, but it's bulky and adds weight. I picked up a small water filtration device from EMS that will filter out 99 percent of the world's bacteria, which really means 100 percent but they say 99 to cover their butts in a lawsuit. I bought it when I was getting ready to go to Africa for the Peace Corps and the guy told me it would filter *that* water. It was $40 and comes in a pack smaller than a poncho.

8. First Aid Kit
   There are sharp things on the boat. We have all seen hooks in the hand, or knife cuts. All you really need is some iodine, bandages, tape, and sterile gauze pads. Oh, and um, FYI, the iodine is gonna hurt a little bit.

9. Rain Gear
   This might sound silly, but if you're dry, you won't burn as many calories or make as many mistakes. Rain gear isn't just for rainy days, it's also for big waves. As an added bonus, most of the stuff that's made today is windproof too. I wear my Aero and Nano all the time. And the Strykr will actually float you if you fall in (kids, don't try that at home).

10. Life Jacket
    Not just any life jacket. You need one that fits. The one in your boat that belongs to your kid might not be the best thing to rely on should you need it. Not only that, places like the Susquehanna have *huge* fines for periods of the year if you're not wearing one (during the winter to early spring). This is not out of a big need to want you to be safe, but more out of a desire to not waste taxpayer's money on hiring a dive team to find you when you fall in a 35°F river.

Without the author's Stormr suit in Minnesota he would have had a much harder time catching these giants at Mille Lacs.

11. Ziploc Bags

    This is the best way to keep your phone, wallet, license, extra keys, and other personal items safe and dry. And it costs about $0.10.

12. Maps

    Graphs will go out. Electrical devices are bound to fail in the water. Having a paper map can be the difference between finding your way to safety and floating into darkness. Pairing them with a cheap compass will at least show you which way is north if you get turned around in the dark and lose your way. It's also a great idea to update your nautical cards for your graphs so that you have the most recent information on where you're going. The last thing you want to do is hit something at top speed because you thought you were driving in a safe area. This is also very important at places like Douglas Lake, in Dandridge, Tennessee, where they can lower the water so much that you'll see giant islands in the fall, in places you were running 70 mph in the spring.

13. Sun Protection

    I don't wear sunscreen. I don't like the scent it leaves on the bait, it's messy, and it doesn't work. The day I met John McGoey we were fishing the Potomac River. I applied at least three bottles during that day on the water and I still burned. UV clothing is much better. Get a buff for your face, gloves for your hands, and a long-sleeved shirt. All of this is breathable and won't make you feel like you're dressed for winter in July.

14. Jumper Cables, Fuses, and WD-40

    You might not realize it, but you can do a lot with jumper cables. If your cranking battery dies, you can use the jumper cables to start the motor off your trolling motor batteries. Once the motor is running it will charge that cranking battery, and you'll be good to go. Just to make sure, you should drive a bit and limit your use of the other batteries until you're sure the battery is charged up. The WD-40 will help clean the terminals if needed, and is rumored to be a good attractant for smallmouth. I'll neither confirm nor deny. And as for fuses, they blow all the time, and you will not find a NAPA in the middle of Lake Ontario. Ever.

15. Some Good Reading

    Bring this book with you. You never know when you might need it!

3

Unlocking the Mystery

The first thing you need to know about smallmouth bass is that they love current. This is the major difference between them and their green cousins the largemouth. They'll search for it, and when they find it, that's where you'll find them. Now I know that many people think that in large bodies of water there is no current; that's a huge misconception. In fact, the bigger the lake, the more current you will find. For instance, Lake Ontario is massive, and on calm days (which are incredibly rare) you could certainly drive your boat to places where you could sit and not move for hours. Even that giant body of water has a main channel, with a current that's so subtle you might not notice it at the top, but I promise you that if you try to drop shot with a lightweight in that area, you'll see that it still moves before it reaches the bottom. Simply put: all things are relative, so even current that's only moving at 0.5 mph is still enough to attract smallmouth if there's nothing else nearby. Smith Mountain Lake is another prime example of this, and the reaction that the smallmouth there have in response to the dam pulling water is significant, in that they'll move from their roaming areas to the main channel and stage there until the turbines cease and the current dissipates.

In addition to current, smallmouth are also rock stars. When I'm fishing in lakes, I typically look for groups of what resemble big brown bowling balls, with tiny pieces of white shells broken up and scattered in between. It's also very important that you not have slimy algae. For instance, in Chaumont Bay at Lake Ontario there are several smaller bays such as Three Mile Bay. Early in the season this is a great place, but by the end of July the slimy algae has usually arrived, and the fish will vacate until it dies about four weeks later. When this happens the fish will return, and the slimy algae will appear in a different section of the lake that it wasn't in before. If you want to do a quick check you can toss a tube and see what you bring up from the bottom. This is not to be confused with algae bloom. Algae bloom is when the water is filled with tiny green dots, which is why it's often referred to as "pea soup." When I first experienced this I thought that the fish were going to hate it, and I scrambled to find water without it. Then I had a conversation with John McGoey and he told me that it's a psychological glitch for anglers. John said that it's fishermen who think that algae bloom is

Susquehanna River. Anthony Lorefice

bad, and that smallmouth actually love it. This took me some time to wrap my head around, but I have found that it is a mind game to some extent. If you're not getting bites, you can convince yourself that it's the bloom, quickly reach panic mode, and start running to find other water. But that's not necessarily what you should do.

Smallmouth fishing is not easy. Largemouth are so predictable. Pound the banks with jigs, flip docks, pitch grass. They're big and dumb. Smallmouth will break your heart. That's why it's so important to stay focused, to not give up, and to not get so fixated on a bait or pattern that you put yourself in a ditch that you can't get out of. I'll give you two examples of what I mean. In 2011 I was competing in the division championship in New York at Oneida Lake. At the end of day one I was in sixth place and my best friend was in seventh. I had a solid game plan and had a lot of fish (I specifically left them for day two, rather than beat them up on day one). Day two, first thing in the morning I run to my spot, and sure enough there are about ten other boats that magically appeared there. This is a common thing in tournament fishing, where the guys who do well one day will suddenly have a lot of company the next day. It pissed me off a little, but I wasn't too worried because I knew I was on a unique pattern (Hula Grub) and there were a lot of fish there—at least there were at the end of day one. Day two it was a ghost town and at noon I had a big fat zero. By 1:00 PM I still had nothing and I was in full-blown freak-out mode. I decided to make a long run to the other end of the lake, which was a huge gamble because I was leaving a place I knew had produced just a day ago to cross my fingers and hope with less than two hours to go. I got there and struck out for forty-five minutes. With fifteen minutes to go I grabbed my favorite crankbait, boated nine fish, ran back to weigh in and finished in third place. My buddy had stayed behind in that honey hole from day one, and finished with a zero, falling from seventh to fortieth place. Should you always run? No. That spot could have just as easily turned on the minute I left, and he would've reaped the reward for staying the course all day. Because that's how it goes. Sometimes you need to get just one bite to ignite the entire school into a massive feeding frenzy.

And sometimes you need to know when to put down that bait and go to something else. Which brings me to my second example: I've become really fixated on swimbait fishing. In this book you're going to read countless tips about this bait or this presentation. As I wrote this I started thinking about how cyclical my bait selection seems to be in terms of baits. Four years ago, I was a tube maniac. Before that it was a wakebait, before that a drop shot. And what I mean by that is that there are just years where, for whatever reason, a certain type of bait or presentation will dominate and catch fish of all sizes, most of the time. I was really good at figuring out the pattern, which is what always made Danny and me such a good team (Danny Drake was my tournament partner for almost ten years). Danny had an uncanny ability to find fish, and I would sit down, breathe for five or ten minutes, and then it would just come to me that I should be cranking or dragging a tube or whatever. I could always figure it out, and I wasn't too wrapped up in any one bait. But then I started throwing a swimbait and it ruined me because they'll eat it all the time. If it's hot, cold, sunny, cloudy, windy, calm, raining, humid, it doesn't matter. And because of that, it's really hard for me to put it down. Even as I write this, I know that I've had a lot of success lately on a fluke or double fluke, but I'll still start with a swimbait for the first two hours. Granted, I've caught a ton of fish on this bait, but I'll also be the first to admit that it hasn't produced nearly as well in 2016 as it did in 2015.

I have to force myself to put that bait down right now. I don't know if that will always be

Oneida Lake.

the case, but I do know that sometimes it helps to reflect on what has worked in the past, and revisit it. That's been the biggest benefit that I've gotten from this book—being able to return to some of my old roots. Like a Mepps #4 and a Blue Fox with Super Sonic vibration. Things like this that caught tons of fish for me in the early 1990s that I simply stopped using, but that are still great baits. Stay open to diversity, and trust your gut. That's the key to unlocking the mystery behind each trip.

4

Weather

Simply put, no other factor has a greater impact on smallmouth bass than weather. You might not realize it, but everything you do to target these fish is born from something as simple as the seasons (spring, summer, fall, winter), and grows to the most detailed combination of barometric pressure/wind/cloud cover/water temperature/air temperature/current/visibility that you can imagine. I have studied this to a degree that is beyond anyone else that

Picture taken after filming with The Weather Channel. From left to right: photographer Shane Durrance; angler Jim Root; senior coordinating producer for The Weather Channel, Stephen Neslage.

I've met, and while I have accumulated a fair amount of knowledge on the subject, I'm still learning more information and gathering more data every time I'm on the water. By recording data, you build your own encyclopedia of knowledge that you can expand on to improve every outing.

The first question most people ask me relates to how/when/why I started keeping my weather journal. A good friend of mine is a very successful hunter and he told me that using a weather journal really helped him understand migratory patterns and behaviors during hunting season. Over time it allowed him to predict where and when game would arrive, to the point that he could almost tell you down to the minute when and where he would get his yearly prize. Around then I also started noticing that other smaller animals like squirrels and birds were feeding heavily during certain weather conditions. Midway through my second year of keeping this journal with him and the guys at our camp a light went off in my head, and I knew that this would change things for me on the water forever. When I mentioned this to my grandfather he pointed out that the squirrels were always a great indicator for the trout in the stream. If the squirrels were actively feeding, the fish would be too. I decided to test his theory and returned shortly after I left with a limit of browns 18–20 inches long from a very small stream. So began my fishing journal.

The second question I get about my journal is in reference to it being easy or hard. It's not hard at all. In fact, the only thing that's hard is forcing yourself to do it. Many times when you get home you're tired, you have family to attend to, or you have other pressing things that require immediate attention. As much as possible you should try to take down as many details as you can as they happen. When I catch a fish I make a note of the time and general area. If it's just a small fish, it might be just a mental note. If it's a big fish, I'm going to record as much data as I can right then. The fastest way to do that is with a quick voice recording on your phone. I might say "Just caught a giant, 6-pound smallie, on a Yo-Zuri 3DB Vibe S Tennessee Shad at Shacks, ten feet deep, 2:00 PM, burnin' it." I guarantee you that short recording took less time than I'll spend taking pictures of that fish, and it'll help me get bigger fish than that over time. This will also cut my record keeping time a lot, and will make it less pressing for me to do it the minute I get home.

My journal began with the most data I could find, and focused heavily on barometric pressure. Barometric pressure, the common way we refer to atmospheric pressure, is essentially defined as the pressure exerted at any given point by the earth's atmosphere, with a value of 29.92 considered to be the standard or normal level. This number may rise above 31, and may dip below 28, and has huge implications depending on where you are, what season it is, what you're most comfortable doing, and what stage the fish are at in their yearly migratory pattern.

So what is barometric pressure (bp), in a way that's easily understood? Well, think of it like a ceiling in your home. And imagine that there's a certain height in your home that

On set at The Weather Channel, pictured from left to right: Dr. Marshal Sheppard, fishing guide Chris Scalley, and the author. Chad Carhart

you're comfortable with. Would you be comfortable with ceilings that are eighteen feet high? Or would you rather they were seven feet high? Let's imagine that a "normal" ceiling is ten feet, and that you have chandeliers hanging down that are situated perfectly above your head so you don't hit them when you walk from room to room, and switches for those lights on the wall at just the right height for you to reach comfortably. Now imagine that ceiling falls four feet. Now you're hitting your head, you are walking hunched over. You would look for places in your house where the floor was lower, so that you could get back to your comfort zone in your "normal" level. This is exactly how bp impacts smallmouth. And because of their air bladders, the fluctuation in bp can be incredibly discomforting, which is why they will adjust quickly to these changes.

I get a lot of "What's the best kind of pressure for smallmouth fishing?" and my initial response is "I don't know," because that person isn't asking enough questions, and isn't asking the *right* questions. A lot of people will simply say, "Well, the best range of bp is when it's falling from 30 to 29." If you just want a simple answer, then there you go. But if you want a better answer, then you need ask it like this: "I'm really good at fishing slowly, with finesse baits. It's what I'm most comfortable doing. What is the best range of bp during the summer in the Northeast on the Great Lakes to target deep fish in this way?"

Now I could answer that person with a specific range of bp that, combined with a list of other factors, would argue that the best range would be a high level over 30.5 and steady. Why? Because this is when this individual will be most successful. This is the problem with just searching out on the Internet for what is the best range of bp for fishing. You might find a professor in Georgia who found that it's best for bass when it's high and steady, but that individual might have only conducted his research on one lake, that only has a habitat conducive to smallmouth in deep water. Furthermore, that individual might have only done their research in a two-week period, and might not be a very well-rounded angler. If that's the case, as it often is that we have our strengths and preferred techniques, the results would be heavily skewed because you would have no way of knowing if someone else would've had more luck during a particular cold or warm front.

When I build out my weather journal after a trip I go to Weather Underground, and I take a screenshot of the history of the weather for that day, and it looks like this (see next page, top image).

Next I open this screenshot in some sort of editing software, where I have created a template that will allow me to plug in this picture, so that it has a new box below it that's blank. This is where I will mark the fish that I caught with symbols that I've created for myself over time that quickly identify the type of fish, how big it was, and the style I was using when I caught it (power fishing/finesse/reaction bait). Then I can see what else was going on before and after I caught that fish.

Finally, I save that new image (see next page, bottom image), and upload it into my file as a new page where I store the results from each trip and add all the other information: type of lure, color, cloudy, windy, hot, cold, rain, dirty water, etc. Try to use keywords and phrases that are unique and searchable. Depending on what service you use to store your data, there is normally a search box that will let you look for values or keywords. You can search for things like "June" or "25 mph wind." This will highlight all entries with that unique value, and that's a huge advantage when you're getting ready to fish and you have a solid weather forecast. Now instead of guessing when you caught them on that crankbait, you'll be able to

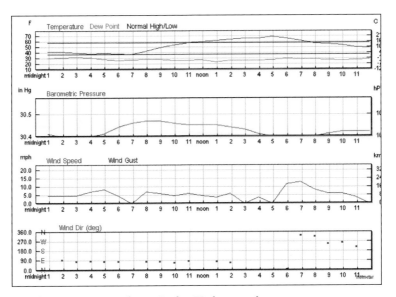

Weather History image from Weather Underground.

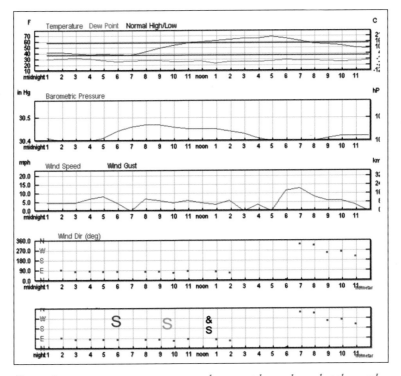

By creating your own system, you can mark your catches and see what the weather was doing at that time.

know exactly and what the conditions were like. Believe me, there's no magic bait that will catch fish the same way 365 days a year. Each bait has a time and place, and documenting your history is the key to unlocking the full potential of each one.

Personally, based on my preferred style(s) of fishing, I am most successful in the summer and fall when the pressure is lower, but that's the opposite for me in the winter and spring. That doesn't mean I don't like other ranges, I certainly do. But like anyone else I have my favorite ways to target smallmouth and these conditions complement those strengths of mine very well. I'm also constantly learning, and with every new technique or strategy that I learn there's a new range of pressure to look at to help me find out when this bait or presentation will be most enticing for the fish. In each section following I will tell you what types of weather conditions I have found to be most ideal for each presentation, but please only use that as a guide. The best information is the kind you curate yourself, and the longer you do this, the better you'll get at being able to pattern and predict where the biggest fish are located.

5

Find the Hive

When I tell people to find the hive, or that I'm "in the nest" it means I've located that school of big fish and I know what bait they want, and how they want it presented. It's actually a phrase coined by my buddy Matty's dad, a.k.a. "The Doctor." He said it one day when we were in the middle of catching over a hundred fish in just three hours, none smaller than 2 pounds and many were over 5. We laughed so hard when he said it, but the more we fished,

One of the best days of smallmouth fishing the author ever had.

the more we said it too, and it just made sense. "Find the Hive" is more than just a saying, it's a science. Rate of fall, light levels, time of day, time of year, depth, wind, retrieval speed, angle of retrieve, bait color, bait scent, temperature (both air and water), water clarity, any or all of these things can play a huge role in determining what you're trying to find, which is not just a school of big fish. You want a school of actively-feeding fish. So while it's true that you can have pieces of that equation put together enough to catch some, it's when it all comes together that you can really smash 'em.

Finding the hive is a lot easier to do if you work together as a team. Until you know exactly what the fish want, you should be using different baits and presentations. This can be difficult to do because it'll force you to keep doing something different even when the guy next to you has caught a couple and you haven't. You want to be careful not to jump on the bandwagon too soon for what will end up being a couple of isolated cases. You need to be sure that you know. Once you know, then you attack them from all sides. What you can do is eliminate certain presentations quickly. For instance, if I'm throwing a reaction bait (spinnerbait, crankbait), my partner should be using something on the bottom (a jig, Senko). If I don't catch anything, but my partner gets to ten, then it's time to switch and throw something on the bottom, but not the identical bait. I'll throw a tube, or a drop shot, or a shaky head. Also, if the season is open, toss a couple fish in your livewell and leave them there for a couple hours while you drive around. This should cause the fish to spit up whatever they've been eating which can tell you a lot about what the forage is. Not just the type, but the color. I've had several days on the water that went from okay to incredible after I saw a crayfish in my livewell that was orange, which is pretty different from the green one I had been using. The more closely you're able to "match the hatch" the more likely it is you'll catch them.

The other essential piece to finding the hive is also the simplest: time on the water. If I have three days, that's usually more than enough time to put the puzzle together. By the end of the first day, if nothing else, I've figured out where they *aren't* and what they *don't* want, but I will usually end on a high note. I've caught some good fish and I have a solid game plan for the next day. Day two is usually go time. I use what I learned the day before and by noon I have them dialed in and the next four to seven hours are pretty magical. Day three is usually just an attempt to use the fine-tuned knowledge from days one and two to try to find one giant fish before I leave. If you think of it as a puzzle, and give yourself that time to unlock it without feeling the pressure to catch them every second, you'll do really well. I also caution against travelling too much on the first day. Pick a location that has a little bit of everything: shallow water, rocks, points, deep areas, grass, whatever that body of water has to offer. Dissect each area, and once you have found them you can target other areas that meet the same criteria. Resist the urge to run all over the lake. You'll waste time and gas, and you'll probably end up targeting the same areas, which will only deliver the same results.

Sunrise in Michigan with Mark Zona.

The only exception to this rule is when you're fishing deep. For instance, there's a shoal outside of Dunkirk on Lake Erie that you could fish without a fish finder because it'll be covered with boats. The reason is because, aside from this shoal, there's nothing around for miles, so thousands of fish will congregate there. In places like that, where you're fishing in deep water and targeting fish that are on the bottom, a good set of electronics will tell you if there are fish there or not. I have been using Humminbird since I started, and their new Helix units require almost no setup and are good to go right out of the box. Meaning you don't need to take a class or be a computer programmer to use them. In this situation, with the proper equipment, you can and should move around. If you don't see any fish on your graph, you should leave. Drive slowly until you mark them, then try the different baits until you're able to catch them quickly.

On the next page is a picture and an example of what I mean. Look at what I'm doing. Each cast covers a different area, and together we are fanning out all around us. Now you're probably saying, "Can't those fish see or hear your bait?" and you're right, especially if I'm using a crankbait or something that produces noise, they certainly can hear it. But often smallmouth will position themselves a certain way and only eat a bait if it's been presented at a particular angle at a particular rate of speed, at a certain depth, etc. Case in point: if you look at the picture below, cast number five is the exact angle that I was catching all my fish on at Simcoe when I sacked five fish that went over 30 pounds total, including one 7-pound

Aerial view of fan casting.

tank. That angle, combined with the speed with which we were drifting, and of my retrieve, put the bait in the hive and generated the strikes from the big fish that my buddy Matty couldn't get. All of my fish came from that angle. And every fish in the livewell that day was my catch.

6

Electronics

There is no doubt that one of the biggest keys to being able to catch smallmouth bass all year long is to have electronic fish finders as well as a serviceable knowledge of how to use them. The fish finders of today are remarkable. Why are these units so important? Well, for starters smallmouth aren't as predictable as largemouth (that's a point I'm going to make many times). It's really quite easy to target largemouth simply by pounding the bank with a jig or flipping docks. While it's true that smallmouth will also be found in these areas from time to time, they spend the majority of their lives in deeper water, in and around offshore structure that is often not something you can locate from up above. For instance, later on there's a chapter about Lake Champlain where I mention two giant fish that I catch 25 feet beneath the surface, off a rock pile that's smaller than my boat. Without my graph there is absolutely no way I would have found that spot. And if I did happen to come across it accidentally, it would be almost impossible for me to find again. Luckily, though, there are numerous options now that make fish finders affordable to people on nearly any budget. Depending on the features you need, you can spend as little as $99 or as much as a few thousand.

I have always used Humminbird electronics. While they have always been regarded as the most reliable, the complaint

Humminbird Helix 12 Units mounted on the dash make finding smallmouth a lot easier.

about them for years was that they were too hard to operate for a novice user. Today's Helix units are really easy to use. You basically can install them on the boat right out of the box, turn them on, and they'll function exactly as they should and do everything you need them to do. And if you're not sure about the installation process, Doug Varenburg is a friend of mine with a YouTube channel that is a really great resource. Doug does a great job of walking people through each process of install, and going over all the functions of each unit, of which there are many. There are nautical charts that are updated regularly to show you the depths from an aerial view. If your lake or river that you're fishing isn't one that has been charted, you can quickly chart it yourself and within minutes you'll have all the contour lines you need. Some of the other cool features they have are side imaging, down imaging, 2-D and 3-D sonar, split screen view, and the newest and coolest is the 360. The 360 unit mounts on the trolling motor and does just what it says; it scans a full 360 degrees with a screen that resembles a clock with a moving hand that scrolls around and around constantly. This is an incredible feature for offshore fishing because it allows you to follow those schools of fish that are moving while chasing big balls of baitfish. Before, if you caught one and had to spend a few minutes fighting the fish, you could come off your spot and need to spend some time trying to relocate it. Now you can simply look and see where they've moved. It's almost cheating, but if you're trying to catch the biggest smallmouth in the world you need every advantage.

If you can't afford to spend hundreds or thousands of dollars, there's a new option that is really pretty great. It's called the iBobber from ReelSonar; it looks like a bobber and it's meant to be casted with a rod and reel but you can also just tie it off the side of the boat if you want. I use this a lot when I'm fishing water that is too small for my big boat, or simply won't allow big motors, when shore fishing, or wading. The cool thing about this is that it pairs with your smartphone via bluetooth, and it has a ton of features that you get in those high-priced units. It's also got a fish calling ability similar to that of the Hydrowave, that really works well for smallmouth when the fish are primarily feeding on shad and other baitfish. This unit has an internal battery that you charge with a USB plug. If you're just looking to be able to mark fish and/or structure without having to spend a ton of money, this is the perfect unit. What I like best about it is that

iBobber Pulse comes with the Siren fish call technology and connects directly to your phone or tablet via bluetooth smart technology.

every time I've marked fish with it, it's proven to be fish. That to me is the biggest key to the success of any fish finder. It has to accurately mark the fish. This thing is really cool though because you can use it anywhere. I've even attached it to paddle boats. If you're going to be fishing offshore you need a way to identify fish. If you pair this with the Navionics app for your phone, you can have contour lines and fish marking ability for under $200, and you can take it anywhere.

7

Become a Bird Watcher

———

When people talk about Oneida Lake you hear a lot of people mention "following the birds." What they're talking about are terns, and an awesome phenomenon that can yield huge results. These are small white birds, with black heads and orange beaks. Terns travel in groups and make a very distinct squawking sound. Following them or chasing them can be very productive, but can also be incredibly frustrating. To do so requires a little knowledge, a little luck, and a tiny bit of guesswork. To begin with, don't chase just one. In fact, I don't investigate unless I see at least ten birds, very chatty, diving in the water. When they do this, they'll actually tuck their wings and dive head first at full speed from high in the air, and slam into the water. What's happening is the smallmouth are in a school, on a school of baitfish, and they're chasing the baitfish to the surface. The birds see this, and it's like they announce it to the world. If it's not a false alarm, a lot of birds will show up in a short amount of time.

The tricky part is that the bait don't stay put. They're running for their lives, and moving incredibly fast. If you see a large flock of birds diving from high above and crashing into the water at full speed, and start your motor and drive to where they are, they'll be gone by the time you get there, having moved as much as 100 yards in just a few seconds. The key here is trying to guess where they'll go, or getting close enough so that they'll get pushed near you. If you are close enough to see what's going on, you'll be able to witness what looks like boiling water as countless smallmouth bass are splashing at the surface as they chase the baitfish to the top. In fact, the fish are so aggressive that they've actually rammed the bottom of my boat in pursuit of the bait. Most of the time when this happens, the fish will eat anything. But in my opinion a shallow running wakebait or a topwater plug are the two best choices. Whatever you throw you generally want it to be at or near the top, because you don't want the bait to be under the fish.

Yo-Zuri 3DB Pencil, Oneida Lake.

For this reason, I will always have my Yo-Zuri 3DB Pencil tied on and ready. When I see a fish bust on the surface I know I have about seven seconds to get my bait in or around that spot. If I can do that, there's a really great chance that fish will hit again. This is a floating lure, and to properly work this bait you need a stiff rod, fairly long, fast-action, with a fairly high-speed reel. I like to use flipping rods for this application because often times you need to make up a lot of ground from far away and you don't need to let the fish eat it like you do a frog. I pair this with a high-speed reel like a 7.1:1 or higher reel with either braid or 20 lb monofilament line. With two large, exposed treble hooks, you should set the hook the minute the fish bites the bait. Once the bait hits the water I wait a couple seconds then start slowly reeling it in while I work the rod in a motion that is down and to the left with short strokes. This will make the lure dart from side to side on the top, in what is commonly referred to as a "walk the dog" motion. This can be an incredibly exciting way to fish, because the smallmouth will behave like sharks on occasion, swimming full speed and ramming the bait from below, propelling it high into the air. When smallmouth do this, it's because they see the lure as a wounded fish and they're trying to stun it. When this happens, let the bait fall back to the surface and let it rest for about five seconds, then just give it a soft tug and leave it again. The best days and times for this bait are late spring/summer/early fall, on cloudy/overcast days, with slight wind.

8

Rivers

When you think of smallmouth you should immediately be thinking of current. Smallmouth bass love current. Not to the point of whitewater rapids, but they will seek it out as their preferred location in rivers. How much current depends on each body of water, but typically in river charts I like it to be over four and under six. This range is great because it's not moving too fast or slow, but it will keep the fish where you can easily find them, and they'll be eating. Because river smallmouth are constantly fighting current, they burn a lot more calories than lake fish, which will require them to eat more frequently. While many will still eat bigger baits in rivers, downsizing can often lead to a lot more fish. This is especially true in colder water, because eating a giant meal can make them sluggish and they need to operate on a higher energy level. While it's common for me to use the same size hardbaits, I usually use a much smaller tube or jig in rivers.

Many lakes, Ontario included, have tributaries where fish will congregate during certain times of year.

When analyzing a river you want to find bends, drop offs, submerged trees, rocky areas, transitions, and most importantly you want to fish the edges. When the current is moving and the water level is normal or above normal, it will push those smallmouth to the bank and make them very easy to find. Find a relatively deep hole for that body of water, drive to the top, drift downstream so not to burn up your trolling motor batteries, and work from the bank out. Staying as far away from the shore as you can while still able to reach it with your lure, you should get bit within the first eight feet from the water to the bank. This is a great place to work a reaction bait, something white or bright colored, and flashy. Spinnerbaits and swimbaits are my two favorite baits in this location and I'll tell you how to work them later on.

When the water is low the fish spread out, and they can be harder to find. Sometimes they'll be grouped up in and around deeper holes or in the bend itself, but not always. In the dog days of summer when the water temperatures are higher, you'll want to find the deeper holes. While I've said that smallmouth love current, they don't love hot water in the summer and will leave the current for cooler temperatures. These deeper holes, bridge pilings, and points are where you'll find those groups of summer smallies. Also pay attention to any irregularities you might find. A small creek, even if it looks like just a trickle, will often have at least one or two good smallmouth beside it. A handful of rocks on the shore might lead to a giant rock pile under the surface and shouldn't be neglected simply because you don't see a bend or a downed tree. I see things like this as prime locations to pick up one or two fish.

Chenango River smallmouth.

Think about that, if next time you go out in your river and you hit a dozen spots like that and get one or two smallies off each one, then you caught twenty or thirty fish that you wouldn't have. And you still have your favorite holes to hit. These subtle differences are why I am able to catch over fifty smallmouth in a day on a place like the Chenango River and tell everyone what I caught them on, only to have people call me two days later and say they only caught five. The little things add up.

You also won't find the same fish in the same places every time you fish a river. Smallmouth are some of the most nomadic creatures on the planet, with some studies suggesting they can swim over thirty miles a day. The key is to look and pay attention to things that are different. Transitions are key in rivers.

9

Lakes

This can be tricky, and is part of the reason why fishing for smallmouth bass can frustrate a lot of people. I want you to try to forget everything you've been told about needing to look for smallmouth in deep areas with rocky bottoms. Just because this is how things have always been done, doesn't mean it's how things should continue to be done. Smallmouth are rarely in these areas during the spring, summer, and fall because there's no reason for them to be there. Think about it from the most basic level of need: nourishment. Smallmouth need to eat just like you or me. Not only that, but they want to eat the best food available, and that food isn't necessarily at the bottom of the lake. Take a place like Oneida, for example. Some of the biggest smallmouth I've ever caught in that lake came from a grassline when I was targeting largemouth. I caught a 3.5-pound largemouth, and caught a 3.5-pound smallmouth on the very next cast, off the same submerged piece of grass. The more I fished that area, the more I found that the big largemouth and smallmouth in that lake were living together. Not the largemouth that are under docks, but the schooling fish in 7–12 feet of water.

The other factor that you need to take into consideration when fishing these lakes is the presence of algae bloom in the summer. In some of the worst cases, the water will look like pea soup and there might even be ordinances in effect that prohibit swimming. For a lot of anglers, the site of algae bloom is like a death sentence, but it's only a hindrance to the angler. Smallmouth love algae bloom. This is the exact opposite of what we've been programmed to think when it comes to fishing; we've been conditioned to feel the need to find clean water because we believe that fish will seek that out. But algae bloom is not dirty water in the eyes of a smallmouth, so they won't be fixated on finding cleaner water like they would if there was a rain storm. What you have to do is forget the million green dots you see, and don't let it get in your head that you can't catch them there. If that happens then you're beat, because if you tell yourself you won't catch them then you won't.

Oneida Lake. Russ Scalf

As far as rain and dirty water, there is no place I have ever been where this is more evident than Maple Bay on Oneida Lake. If we get half an inch of rain, that bay will be chocolate milk the next day. Whenever you have a creek of that size that empties into a bay the way this one does, you're going to have that dirty water pushing out into the lake. When this happens, the bay is incredibly tough to fish, and it's really not worth the effort. However, the good news is that normally you can find a transition area that is very well defined, almost like a straight line, like you would see if you were looking at a container holding oil and water. And this is where the fish will be, waiting for their food to come from that dirty water with zero visibility into the cleaner water. It's also a great place for them to get out of the direct sunlight.

But creeks like that can be dynamite places to find smallmouth in the spring and fall. For example, Big Bay Creek at Oneida has a phenomenon that takes place in April where the swamp that feeds the lake can produce water with temperatures to nearly 80°F when the main lake water is still just above 50°F. This happens when the growth in the swamp is low, and the sun is shining. The sunlight generates a lot of heat on the shallow water in the swamp (approximately 2 inches), and with the right kind of wind that hot water will get pushed out towards the main lake. As the day goes on that tract of warm water acts like a magnet for all species of fish, including smallmouth. By late afternoon/early evening there will be thousands of fish in that creek with metabolisms that have skyrocketed from the dramatic temperature increase and they'll act ravenous. If you can match the food source you can easily catch a hundred fish in just three hours and most of them will be heavy from the winter feed.

In the fall you won't see this same level of temperature diversity, but you will still see tremendous amounts of feeding activity in the creeks and creek mouths. Shad will run into these areas in droves; remember that the smallmouth follow them all year as one of their primary food sources, and this is no exception.

Now when I am fishing at Oneida I am rarely, if ever, deeper than 15 feet and most of the time I'm in that 7- to 12-foot area. In the spring, the smallmouth can key in on very specific depths in that range, and by that I mean that they're only in 7–8 feet. They'll stay there for a couple weeks, then they'll move out and be in just 11–12 feet. This is why having great electronics is so crucial. With my new Humminbird units, I can highlight an area like that 7- to 8-foot range, color code it red, and it'll light up every area of that lake that is 7–8 feet deep. Then I can tell just by looking at the map all the places that should hold fish during

Oneida Lake. Russ Scalf

this particular outing/time of year. This saves me a ton of time, which gives me more time to spend catching. This specific depth is critical to your success, and you won't find them outside of that range with the exception of a few roamers that are transitioning.

The exception to the rule of depth that I follow in lakes is for the Great Lakes, or for bodies of water that have been infested by gobies, or that are man-made and have dams that will periodically pull water. The goby is an invasive species that is spreading across all our freshwater and saltwater in North America. This is such an important topic when it comes to smallmouth bass that I have reserved an entire chapter to explain their existence in our waters and how this impacts the way we target smallmouth.

The dams change everything completely, and you have to be able to know when to expect current and how much. Most places, like the TVA (Tennessee Valley Authority) has an app that you can download for free that will tell you the schedule for places like Douglas Lake. The thing to keep in mind is that this is just a schedule that can and often does change. In other places like the Susquehanna River, there are dams where water will even be backfed from time to time, which can disrupt the smallmouth entirely. Smallmouth in these lake systems are married to the current that is generated by the dams in a manner slightly similar to tidal fishing. Simply put: the more current you have, the better your chances. That goes for outward moving water, or for warm water discharges that are spilling in.

10

Seasons

I love spring smallmouth bass fishing because I am sick and tired of the cold! Living in Upstate New York for the majority of my life, you would think that I've learned to love the winter. That is absolutely not the case. In fact, the older I get, the more and more I despise cold weather. Smallmouth fishing in the spring can be incredible, which also contributes to my love for it. The fish are really aggressive; for the most part they're heavy from having binge-fed all winter, and the warm days make for increased feeding activity leading up to the spawn.

Each season is drastically different, but cyclical at the same time. You have to imagine a circle with arrows, like you see in a recycling symbol, that depict motion around and around. That's what happens with smallmouth bass migratory habits. Each season is a migratory pattern, or stage, that is replicated later on. Shallow, deep, shallow, deep. Spring, summer, fall, winter.

SPRING: BEFORE, DURING, AND AFTER THE SPAWN

The spawn is your best shot at a trophy smallmouth because the fish are really heavy, and they're incredibly aggressive. These stages of reproduction are often referred to as prespawn, spawn, and post spawn. When each stage begins depends on water temperature, air temperature, and moon phase. In southern areas, the spawn will generally take place during the full moon in April. However, in northern bodies of water like New York and Canada, it's not uncommon to find smallmouth bedding in June or July. The better you understand these stages, the more likely it is that you'll be able to catch the fish of a lifetime.

Prespawn

Prespawn is an incredible time of year. In my opinion, the last week of June at the St. Lawrence River is the best freshwater fishing in the world, and there are many other anglers who share that same feeling with me. I say this not only because it's prespawn there, but also

Chenango River smallmouth.

because there are two counties in New York State that don't allow catch and release for small-mouth and they are Jefferson and St. Lawrence. Those two counties cover the Eastern Basin of Lake Ontario and The St. Lawrence River. This means that from December 1, when the season closes, until the third Saturday in June the following year, it is illegal to target small-mouth bass, and the local law enforcement officials in those areas have no sense of humor about this regulation. That means you take one of the most aggressive fish and give them a break for almost eight months, so it's really no wonder why these fish are in such a feeding frenzy when the season opens.

What begins this prespawn stage is when the first wave of smallmouth move from their wintering holes to the outskirts of the shallow bedding areas. Now in most regions, this area is the first ledge in relation to their deeper winter abodes, but there are exceptions to that. In Buffalo, for example, on Lake Erie, the smallmouth have been known to spawn in 40–50 feet of water. In nearby Lake Ontario the fish are in a much more predictable and visible area of crystal clear water 8–10 feet deep. If you're having trouble finding where this migratory point is, see if you can find out some information from local experts on where the fish winter, and get a good nautical chart. From there you want to find the areas that have drop-offs near shallow flats. This ledge will be a great place to look for prespawn smallmouth. The fish move into this prespawn location two weeks away from a full moon when the water temperature is in the high 40s or low 50s.

This is without a doubt my favorite time of year to fish for smallmouth. Not only are the fish aggressive, but it's a powerfishing bonanza, which is really my favorite way to fish. That means swimbaits, crankbaits, drop shots, spinnerbaits, A-rigs, lots and lots of chucking and winding. Sadly, this time of the year is fleeting, and once the fish move out of this stage the fun is over for months. You can still catch them, but they need weeks and weeks to put their weight back on, so there's a period of time when it's difficult to catch a fish over five pounds.

What's also really great about the prespawn is how easy it is to find the fish. What I do is look for those ledges, and position my boat so that I can drift down and cast parallel with them. Most people make the mistake of putting themselves in the right location, but casting at the shore instead. When you do this, your bait is only in the hive for the last few feet of the retrieve, and the only fish you're going to catch are the ones that have moved up early, or that are right on top of your bait before you take it out of the boat. If you cast down the ledge, parallel to the shore, you'll have your bait in the strike zone the entire time, increasing your catch rate tremendously because this is where the majority of the fish will be during this early prespawn stage.

Now once they've moved in and started to look for places to make beds, that's when you want to start concentrating your casts in the direction of the shore. But what you don't want to do is run right in and beat the bank. Start out in deeper water, do a drift, and then move in a bit and drift it again, and keep repeating this until you find where the fish are. When I'm fishing for prespawn fish at Oneida I start on the shoals first thing in the morning and I work a topwater bait. But after that I go to my ledges that have adjacent flats and I start in twenty feet of water and cast in towards the shore. If I don't get good numbers of fish I'll move in so my boat is in fifteen feet and cast in towards the shore. I'll keep moving in like that, not necessarily in increments of five feet, but in stages relative to my casting distance. If I'm able to cast forty yards, then I'm going to move in twenty yards each time, so that I'm certain that I'm covering every inch of water during my search.

What I have found is that the fish during the prespawn will tend to be in very specific depths like fourteen feet, eleven feet, and seven feet. This is so important because if they're in seven feet and you drift off into eight feet, you won't catch them. You have to have your bait exactly where they are. No other time of year will be as depth specific as this one, but don't see it as a negative. Use this to your advantage and absolutely drill them once you figure it out.

This is also a time of year when it is more important than any other (in my opinion) to match the hatch in order to have the best days. Yes, they're overly aggressive during prespawn, and yes, you can use just about any jerkbait or crankbait or swimbait and catch fish.

But there are definitely advantages to using particular baits and that's why it is so important to keep trying different baits until you find one that you're absolutely drilling them on. I learned this back in 2012 during a trip to Erie with Larry. The lake slicked off at noon and it was calmer out of Buffalo than I had ever seen it before. Not an ounce of wind. So we packed up and headed into the Niagara River. When we got there, we started throwing our drop shots and we were catching a couple here and there, but then I noticed that one of our fish had spit a small minnow on the deck. I picked it up and looked it over, and immediately I knew that it looked exactly like a Lucky Craft Bevy Shad in Gun Metal that I had brought. I tied it on and caught a giant on the first cast. Then another, and another, and another. Not only that but they were crushing it, really hard. That's when you know you're really dialed in, when they're not just biting, they're choking the bait. I had an extra and gave one to Larry and we set the world on fire for the rest of the day. That bait won't always produce like that, but I know that I need to bring it when I fish the Niagara River in April.

The Spawn

Once the fish move from the prespawn phase into the spawning phase things get weird. For starters, the fish don't all get on beds at once. So you can still catch some prespawners that'll have you wondering if the prespawn is over or not. Just because the water temp climbs to the right zone and the moon is full, doesn't mean all the fish will spawn at once. There are waves of fish, similar to the way that does (female deer) become ready at different times. I would say, though, that the full moon in May is normally when most of the fish will spawn if the water temp has risen high enough (above 50°F). But the farther north you go, the later in the year that will happen. At Simcoe in Canada, the best time of year is the first week in July. So the best way to plan your trips is to first know the regulations about targeting fish, have access to the water temperature, and to pay close attention to the lunar calendar.

When they do spawn and they're on beds, where they'll be is different for each body of water. At Ontario and Oneida and places like that, they're in 8–15 feet, and your best bet is to drag a tube. At Erie, depending on where you are, they could be super shallow, or they could be forty feet deep. At Smith Mountain Lake in Virginia the key is to look for banks with red clay; the fish will be in fifteen feet and you can pick them apart one by one with a drop shot.

Once the fish get on beds it's a different ballgame. In an appearance on The Weather Channel I made the comment that ". . . anyone who said the fish weren't biting was telling an untruth that was created by fishermen to make themselves feel better because they didn't catch anything that day." But what was cut from that comment was the exception that I pointed out to what is known as "bed sickness." When smallmouth get locked on to the mating cycle, there is about a one- or two-day window in which they will eat very

Oneida Lake. Russ Scalf

little, and because they're really shallow (less than 3 feet), they can see you. If they do happen to see you, then there's almost no way they're gonna eat. Especially the big ones. Remember that when you're fishing in really clear water. If you can see them, they can definitely see you.

When I was at Ontario with Brett Forester we filmed a smallmouth on a bed. She was a big female, and highly aggressive. In fact she even tried to chase Brett away. Brett filmed me catching her in what we believed to be the first actual recording of a smallmouth eating a drop shot in a non-captivity setting. But that took almost an hour, and I didn't have the patience for it. (There's more about that day later on.) So will they eat when they have bed sickness? Yes. Will they do it while they can see you? Yes. Is it easy? Hell no. I don't have the patience to work a fish for an hour. I'd rather spend that time looking for fish that aren't bed sick.

Bed sickness isn't just a real thing, it's the worst thing. When this happens you'll see huge schools of giant smallmouth shallow, and they won't touch a single thing you throw at them. In fact, you could tie your entire tackle box on the end of the line and throw it out there and they'd look at everything you had and keep going. This, to me, is one of the most frustrating lessons you'll learn as a smallmouth fisherman. Having to see them ignore everything you offer them is horrible, and that feeling gets much worse when you realize it's not gonna happen and you walk away, knowing that they're there, and enormous. But after that period, before the female drops her eggs, the fish become highly aggressive again because they're competing for her. So what you'll see are maybe as many as six or seven males swimming around one female. These fish are really easy to target, and they'll eat anything that swims within five feet of her. Just don't let the first one come off before it gets to the boat or they'll all swim away.

If they are on beds and they're deep, you need a drop shot, and you need to put it right in their bed, and they'll eat it almost immediately. If they're under twenty feet you can also drag a tube or a jig, but use something compact like a Little D or a D Bomb because you don't want them to be able to pick it up, move it, and then drop it, which is what they're gonna try to do. They don't want to eat every single thing that comes into that area. So make it hard for them to just touch a piece of it and pull it away. I also want to point out that I'm not a fan of targeting fish that are on beds or guarding fry. I don't do it, and I would ask that others not do it either because it puts the future at risk. They're guarding babies, and you won't see an impact in a year, or two years, but you will in ten or fifteen years, and it'll take many years for the species to recover.

Post Spawn

The first couple days immediately following the spawn is the worst time of year to fish for smallmouth. The fish have spent a lot of calories and are incredibly hungry, which is a good thing for fishermen. However, they're exhausted, and want easy meals they don't have to work for. Typically they retreat back to deep water, but in some instances they'll stay shallow (Mille Lacs, for example, is a place where once the fish move shallow to spawn they stay shallow until late summer and then they retreat deep and stay deep through the winter). The fish have recently lost a lot of weight because they weren't eating much while on beds, so it makes it really hard to find bigger fish for the next four or five weeks while they try to put their weight back on.

In the first few days following the spawn there will be a lot of fish shallow, and this is one of the few times you'll be able to catch smallmouth on docks. My favorite bait for that is a wacky rig because it's a great bait that you can work and skip easily, that is also really effective for targeting smallmouth that have been under a lot of pressure. This is not a time to throw a swimbait or anything with noise, especially if you're fishing a high-profile body of water that attracts a lot of smallmouth fishermen. In those bodies of water those fish have seen about ten million swimbaits in the past month, and if you think you're going to present it in a way they haven't seen it, you're nuts. Instead show them a fluke, or a donkey rig, or toss a small drop shot with a 6-inch leader on it (this can be difficult to throw around docks).

Sunset in upstate New York. Russ Scalf

The fish that have moved out deep now offer one of the most thrilling experiences you can ever have as a fisherman. This, more than any other time of year, is when you want to throw a walking bait like a Sammy, or a Yo-Zuri Pencil. What's most exciting is that the fish will actually come up from some really deep depths to hit those baits. Often coming from as deep as 20–30 feet. First thing in the morning is a great time to throw this bait on shoals and reefs. If the sun stays hidden they'll eat it all day. And a little wind is a big help. Four or five weeks after the spawn things will return to normal and the fish get into their warm weather routines. This brings everything back to business as usual. I do a pretty good job of keeping a calendar about the spawn phases, and I've learned that there are particular places that I just want to be at certain times of the year. A few of them are:

Susquehanna River (lower end near Harrisburg, Pennsylvania), first week in April
Lake Erie, Buffalo, second week in April (dependent upon when ice out happens)
Traverse City, third week of April
Candlewood Lake, last week of April/first week of May
Smith Mountain Lake, first week of May

Oneida Lake/Oneida River, second week in May
Lake Champlain, last week of May
Cayuga Lake, second week of June
St. Lawrence River/Eastern Basin of Lake Ontario, third week in June
Lake Simcoe, first week of July

SUMMER

The summer is when I caught my first ever smallmouth, so it has a special place in my heart. Not only that, but it's the only season of the four where you can literally catch the fish anywhere, doing just about anything. This allows you to utilize your strengths, but also refine your weaknesses and improve on presentations and techniques that you're not real confident with, especially when it comes to finesse fishing. Because, while you can power fish your way through summer, you need to be able to use things like a drop shot and a shaky head if you want to be successful because there are days when a 3-inch worm will out-fish a ½ oz. jig.

This time of year is exciting for me because finesse, and offshore deep fishing, are things that I really enjoy. I remember talking to Cliff Pace after he won his first Bassmaster Classic and he told me that if I could learn to fish for schooling fish that it would ruin me forever, like it did him, because he's either a zero or a hero. When you target those fish you're usually alone, because it's a hell of a lot easier to beat the bank, drag a point, or flip a dock than it is to locate deep fish and stay on them, especially smallmouth. The positive side of that is that when you have those kinds of fish all to yourself, you can put together some pretty magical days. And just because the fish are deep or suspended doesn't mean you're limited to just fishing one type of presentation. I've caught summer smallmouth on topwater baits at noon in 25 feet of water when those fish were originally marked on the bottom. I've also seen them busting shad on the surface in 40 feet and caught them on a wakebait or a trap.

What makes the summer so difficult is the fronts and the crazy weather. One day it'll be 100°F, and the next day it'll be 68°F with winds 35–40 knots out of the north. And this is why it's so important to have those finesse skills to be able to catch fish all summer long. Just because the weather sucks, doesn't mean the fishing does. I've spent many summer days in rain gear head to toe, smashing them on a drop shot in 25 feet of water in 6-foot waves, puking all day long from being seasick and refusing to quit because I was on a giant school of 5-pounders. This was my first ever trip to Lake Ontario and I tell this story a lot. It was my birthday (August 11), and I took third place that day with just under 25 pounds of bronze.

But I can't stress enough how nasty the cold fronts can be. Ideally in summer you want long periods of constant weather, because the fish will be easy to pattern and locate, which is

Lake Erie with Larry Mazur. Jon Fuchs

the hardest part of smallmouth fishing. This can be made even more difficult in the summer because the fish can literally be anywhere, in any depth. So while a sharp drop in the barometer will trigger a quick feeding frenzy, it's short lived, and what follows is usually not good for people that don't have a full arsenal of techniques under their belt.

Summer is also the time to flip craws, tubes, and jigs. It's great for chucking spinnerbaits, for cranking, or burning traps. You can catch them on jerkbaits, A-rigs, swimbaits, Carolina rigs, ned rigs, petey rigs, Texas rigs, live bait. The only limitations for bait selection are your weather, your body of water, and your ability to locate the schools. Shoal and reef fishing are key this time of year. The best plan of attack is to use a spinnerbait and drift over them. If you don't get bit, make a second pass with a tube. If it's not too windy and you're marking fish then definitely grab your finesse stuff and go at them that way.

FALL

The fall is legendary. Period. Not because the fish are as big as they are in the spring; they're not. But what the fall offers that no other season can is the potential for an endless marathon of pure insanity on the water. The first hard frost will put the fish in a bit of a funk, but the second one tells them that it's game on and the feeding frenzy begins. This means that in most lakes and rivers, the fish will return to the shallow areas they were in during the spring. In the fall smallmouth eat like they won't see another meal for months. It's not uncommon to catch fish that are so gorged with shad and crayfish that their mouths are overflowing. I've caught fish on a 5-inch swimbait that had 4-inch shad half unswallowed.

As the water temperature drops into the 50s, the drop shot, lipless crankbait, and swimbait bite takes off. But nothing can compare to the effectiveness of an Alabama rig this time of year. Days with heavy winds and rain are ideal for this bait. The key will be finding out if they want a bladed rig or the regular. Most of the time, I start with the blades. Depending on where I am I'll go with as small a rig as a three-wire and up as high as the seven-wire big dog.

Oneida Lake, Oneida River smallmouth. Matt Dolinsky

Throwing this bait isn't just as simple as tying it on, throwing it out, and reeling in schools of giant fish. There's definitely an art to using the bait, and I highly suggest you read the chapter on it in this book before you head out and get hugely disappointed.

But what I love the most about the fall is something I touched on about it having the potential to be an endless slugfest. If the weather holds, and the air temperatures stay in the middle to upper 50s by day, and in the upper 30s at night, this feeding frenzy will continue. In fact, in 2015 the early stages of winter were so mild that I was still on the water in New York on New Year's Day catching eighty-five fish a day with my buddy Matty. Now, granted, that's technically winter, but we were still seeing fall conditions with unseasonably warm days that just continued to see fish holding in that fall feeding pattern. The only reason that the switch gets flipped from the fall feed to wintering is temperature. The best-case scenario is that there's no freeze. If the water temps stay above 45°F, you can have an incredible few months. The reality though is that you're basically praying for more global warming when you're asking for conditions like that.

There are two things you really want to avoid in the fall. The first is dirty water. Smallmouth will avoid that like the plague and they'll travel long distances if they have to. Fall can be notorious for flooding, so you'll want to pick your spots carefully. There's also the danger factor with floods and hazards that you can't see. This is not the time to be navigating unknown water if you can't see where you're going, particularly in rivers.

The second thing you want to be careful of is trying too hard to get any group of fish to eat. This is the fall, it's not the dog days of summer, and you need to run and gun if the fish aren't eating. Don't be your own worst enemy and wait for a group of fish to turn on. This time of year you shouldn't need to work to get fish to eat. The more time you spend on fish that you're not catching, the less time you'll have to catch the fish that are biting in other locations. And this is a real thing. Just because you're on a school of fish on the east end of the lake and they're not biting, doesn't mean that the fish two miles away are in the same state. There can be numerous factors involved beyond your control, and frankly you can never be completely sure that the fish you're marking are even smallmouth. You could be sitting over a school of walleye, or perch for that matter. You could also be around too many baitfish, making it too difficult for the smallies to pick out your bait from a smorgasbord of food options in front of them. Work fast, cover water, find those aggressive fish, and hammer on them while you can.

WINTER

This is the time of year most people dread, especially in the north. Not because the fishing isn't good, but because the weather is horrible, and we often get forced off the water by ice. If not from bodies of water freezing over completely, then by shorelines freezing, launch ramps being inaccessible, and floating chunks of ice that complicate retrieval of baits. Not to mention your guides freezing up, making your ability to cast questionable. There are snowstorms, treacherous travel conditions, shorter days, and the simple fact that your motors should be winterized and put away rather than being operated in sub-freezing conditions. Yet despite all of this, there are days when we can get out on the water and catch a hundred fish, and frankly that's why we do it.

But it's not the same. The fish are lethargic, and they don't fight like they should. They don't eat like they should, and it doesn't feel as great reaching into the water to get them as it should. Furthermore, it's downright dangerous when it's that cold because that's when mistakes are made. And this time of year one mistake can kill you. So be sure to take every precaution if you are going out on the ice or the open water. Every year in and around the Great Lakes we hear stories of people who die unnecessarily. Wear your lifejacket at all times, keep extra dry clothes in the boat always, respect the ice and water, and try not to go alone.

The author and Austin Felix in Minnesota. Matt Dolinsky

When you do go, you're going to be using a lot of spoons, hair jigs, live minnows, and tubes. You're going to be working fairly slowly, and focusing on hard-bottom areas in slow-moving water. You want to look for the deepest water you can find. The fish aren't going to be shallow. They want to find the most constant temperature they can, even if that means being in ninety feet of water. In rivers I typically look in 15–25 feet, with 10 feet being the bare minimum. In really deep lakes like Cayuga, Ontario, or Erie, I'll start in at 35–40, but you'll definitely have fish much deeper than that. However, you have to be really careful when you pull a fish up from over 50 feet too quickly because you can actually cause their air bladders to explode. For that reason I would encourage people not to target fish at this depth.

PART II

Smallmouth Lures and Their Presentation

11

Texas Rigs

This is probably the one presentation that I would guess the majority of people reading this book would say they've used. Texas rigging is something that's been around for a very long time, and most people think they have it all figured out. However, most people are doing it incorrectly, and that's why they aren't catching as many fish as the people in the boat next to them. Like anything else, there are ways to perfect this presentation that will elevate it from just another standard technique, to one that will allow you to systematically pick them off

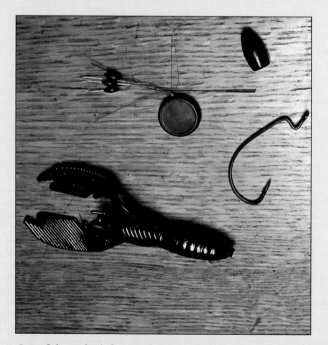

One of the author's favorite baits is a Texas rigged craw, with a pegged weight.

6th Sense bobber stops.

one by one with the precision of an open-heart surgeon. So before we get into that, let's start with the basics. The Texas rig, simply put, is a soft plastic bait that is set up weedless with a bullet weight above the hook. Why is this so deadly on bass? Because it sinks the bait and keeps it on the bottom, while allowing the angler to work it around grass and other vegetation without the worry of snagging, and this is largely where big fish that are near the shore prefer to live.

So to start with you'll want to have a rod that's roughly seven feet long, medium-weight, with a fast or extra-fast tip. Use a high-speed casting reel, and spool it with either 50 lb braid and a leader, or with straight fluorocarbon 20 lb. The key to fishing this bait is whether you peg the weight or not. Pegging the weight refers to using a bobber stop that keeps the weight firmly tucked up against the top of the hook at the bottom of the line near the knot. The bobber stop I use is made by 6th Sense and is very easy to install.

Before you tie on the hook, you make a loop with the line, and pass that loop through one of the loops in the wheel. Slide the bobber stop through the loop, and pull the tag end of your line through. If you're using a real heavy fluorocarbon line you may have a hard time pulling that loop through the stop. In this instance you would feed the line carefully through the stop and then pull it off the wire wheel hoop.

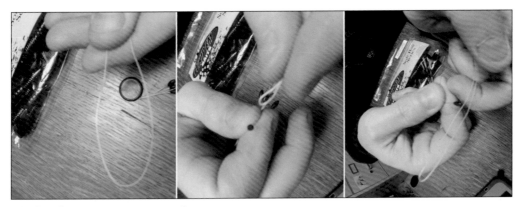

The first three steps to peg your weight.

I don't always peg my weights, and I normally will try to let the fish tell me which way they want it. For weights, I use black or green pumpkin Elite Tungsten bullet weights because they are diamond bored so they don't have inserts (which are garbage) and the diamond-bored hole is super smooth so it won't fray my line. These weights are 97 percent tungsten, while many others are only 70–75 percent tungsten and are made with highly toxic chemicals. I do highly recommend people use these weights, and I urge you not to use lead. Lead is extremely dangerous and can wreak havoc on the entire ecosystem.

When it comes to bait/weight/hook selection you really have a ton of choices, and I'll list mine in order of my personal favorite.

1. Whip 'Em Baits Torpedo Crawdad, Alabama Craw
   I absolutely love using this bait for smallmouth. Drag it across rocks, flip it in grass, or around structure. Texas rigging this bait is key because you will always be using it around things that you'll get hung up on. Use a Trokar TK120 and peg the weight every time. Be sure that you try to slide this bait in the water like an Olympic diver. Practice makes perfect when it comes to that, but the quieter you can be the more hits you're going to get! There are lots of companies and colors to choose from, but if you're in the Northeast you'll want that Alabama Craw or some variation of orange and green that's similar.

2. Bass Pro Shops Magnum Flipping Tube, Junebug
   If I had to guess how many fish I caught on this bait Texas rigged I would first have to guess how many I lost, which would be many. So why then do I keep using it? Because tubes are the number one big bite bait when it comes to smallmouth bass, and there are giant smallmouth that live deep inside big weed beds. If you can't get the tube to the fish without getting snagged, then you don't have to worry about losing the fish because they

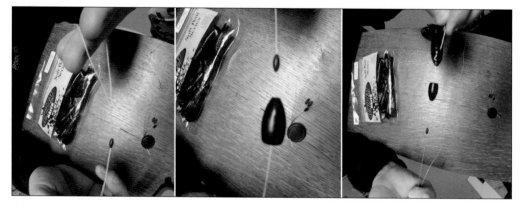

The last steps to peg your weight.

won't bite it to begin with. Get the bite first, worry about landing the fish second. This junebug color is an incredible bait at Oneida, Ontario, and Champlain. I rarely peg the weight with a tube, because I like the added action and the tube will actually float a little bit if I work it fast. I use a ⅜ oz. weight if I'm fishing shallow, and a ½ oz. weight if I'm fishing it over 15 feet.

3. Senko/Rubber Worm
    You really can't go wrong with this bait. I use the 5-inch Senko, and the same low profile hook that I use with the fluke (TK100 3/0) and I'll peg a ¼ oz. bullet weight probably 90 percent of the time. There are times when I will just fish this bait weightless and Texas rigged, especially if it's real hot and the fish are in less than 10 feet of water.

I guarantee you that if you start pegging your weights you'll see an immediate increase in how many fish you catch most of the time. There will be days when the fish will eat the bait better when it's not pegged, but unfortunately you have to use trial and error to find out during those slow days. Also, if you're not sure about how heavy your weights are and

Slowly dragging a Texas rig on the bottom at Oneida. Russ Scalf

want to know if you're using the right size, the bottom of the weight and the top of your soft plastic (where the two meet) should be the same width, so that it looks like one continuous piece from the tip of the weight to the end of the bait. If one is considerably larger than the other you should adjust if you can.

Gear:

7' medium, fast-action casting rod; high-speed reel 7.1:1 or higher; 12 lb KIMURA Jim Root Fishing Fluorocarbon line; Trokar TK130 3/0 hook; Elite Tungsten bullet weight (varying sizes)

Weather:

Spring: Sunny, clear/stained water, water temp 50°F–60°F

Summer: Partly sunny, windy, clear water, water temp 70°F and up, 7–12 feet of water

Fall: Shallow, clear water, any temp.

Winter: Not ideal for winter

12

Jerkbaits

Catching smallmouth is always fun, but when the drop shot bite is hot it can be incredible! The term "jerkbait" or "stickbait" refers to a slender lure with a hard body that resembles a fish. These baits, depending on the size and construction, will generally have either two or three treble hooks on the bottom. I've been using Yo-Zuri jerkbaits for the past twenty years because I think they have the best action, they always swim correctly right out of the

Yo-Zuri jerkbaits are always with the author when he's on the road chasing smallmouth bass.

package (some brands require tuning), and they are incredibly durable. When I first started fishing a lot as a teenager I was obsessed with big predator fish like northern pike and musky and to catch them I wanted the biggest drop shot I could find, and at that time it was a model by Yo-Zuri designed for saltwater fishing. It caught a lot of pike, big pike. And I was incredibly hard on those baits at the time—bouncing them off rocks, ripping them across bridge pilings, not to mention the teeth with which these giant fish were attacking them. But what I also noticed was how many times the smallmouth would eat these baits. Sometimes I would land fish that were smaller than the bait itself. I still carry those saltwater baits (now called the Tobimaru) and they still produce smallmouth. To do it properly requires some basic understanding of a few key elements.

Start by making sure you have the proper gear. To begin with, you want to make sure that you have a stiff fishing rod. This is the most essential part of having a successful drop shot presentation because you need to be able to make the bait dart back and forth; too much give in the rod will make that difficult. For this reason, I do not recommend a glass rod. Instead I like a medium-weight fast-action rod. Because I'm a taller guy (6'-1") I can get away with using a longer rod (I prefer between 7'-6" and 8') that will allow me to cast farther (later on I'll explain why this is important). Next you'll want to have a high-speed reel, something over 7, so you can keep up with the bait during the retrieve, and you'll want to spool that reel with fluorocarbon line. I use between 10–20 lb, depending on where I am and if I'm fishing in current or lakes, or if I'm fishing The Great Lakes or Canada.

When it comes to your presentation, the biggest thing is getting the bait down in the strike zone and keeping it there as long as possible. This is the first reason why it pays to make long casts. When you use a suspending drop shot, which is what you want, the longer cast allows you to have more time in the strike zone between the bait hitting the water and when it returns to the boat. Just like any other bait, there's lead time before you get down to your desired location. The farther you cast, the longer distance you have once that bait is down where you want, increasing the likelihood that you'll get bit. The second reason why you want to make long casts is the inherent benefit of distance. Not only can you cover more water, but smallmouth (particularly in the spring) can be skittish, and the probability of catching fish goes up dramatically if you're not right on top of them.

Jerkbait season is really anytime the water temperature is between 42°F and 55°F. This means that there is a fall and spring season. In either case, the fish could be as deep as 25 feet or as shallow as 5 feet depending on where you are, but that shouldn't change your game plan too much. Why? Because they'll come up, but they'll never go down. So smallmouth on the bottom will swim up 25 feet to hit your bait, but will rarely swim down as little as even 5 feet. So, you make your long cast in an area like I've described. Now what? Well, now you want to make a couple of quick reels to get your bait down a bit, then you want to point the

A beautiful Onondaga Lake smallmouth on the fall drop shot bite! Russ Scalf

rod tip away from you and slightly angled towards the water, and you want to jerk the rod in a downward motion, quickly, like a "snap" or "jerk." You want to repeat this in groups, with varying degrees of pauses in between. Here's a sample of a typical retrieve for me after my bait hits the water:

Five reels
Jerk-Jerk-Jerk
(three-second pause)
Jerk
(half-second pause)
Jerk-Jerk
(two seconds)
Jerk-Jerk-Jerk
(three seconds)
Jerk
(one second)

That's my main drop shot method, and I'll change up the pauses and how violently I'm jerking the bait until I find what they want. But I would say that kind of action will generate strikes 90 percent of the time, with pretty hard jerks. You want that bait to appear to be hurt or dying. Don't be afraid to work the bait in a pool or by the edge of the boat in clear water to get an understanding of how it looks while you're doing it.

Recently I went on the Chenango River and we caught sixty smallmouth in three hours all on drop shots. The water temp was 44°F, the current was 4.5, all normal. The key that day was taking very long pauses in between your succession of jerks. Waiting five to ten seconds and then giving the bait a tiny twitch was the deal. Other times you won't need that pause and the fish will rip it out of your hands while you're working it. Try different angles to the shore, different kinds of jerks, until you find the hive for yourself. So what is the optimum

Chenango River smallie caught on a Yo-Zuri jerkbait.

weather for drop shots? That depends on the season. In the spring and fall it is really good when the water is between 44°F and 52°F. In the late spring/early summer look for sunny days when the air temperature is hot and humid, as this will produce a warming trend that will make drop shot fishing amazing!

Gear:

7' medium-heavy, fast-action graphite or carbon fiber rod (glass rod if fishing in open water); high-speed reel, 7.1:1 or higher; 12 lb KIMURA Jim Root Fishing Tournament Grade Fluorocarbon line

Weather:

Spring and Fall: Water temp 42°F–55°F, clear or dirty water, windy or calm, sunny or cloudy

Summer: Water temp 65°F–90°F, clear or dirty water, calm and sunny

Winter: Not advisable for water temps below 42°F

come up for a bait—they'll almost *never* go down to get it. This is due to the relation of their eyes on their head and their line of sight. Generally I start with 1 foot of leader between hook and weight for every 10 feet of depth I'm fishing in, up to 3 feet of space between hook and weight. So if I'm fishing in 20 feet of water, I'll have two feet of line from my hook to my weight. If I'm in 30 feet or deeper, I'll have 3 feet. This is where I'll start; the fish will tell you what they want. Sometimes fish in 20 feet will want the bait 18 inches off the bottom, and sometimes they'll want it 30 inches. You'll know pretty quick because you shouldn't have to force them to eat. They'll either eat your bait right away, or you won't get bit. If you're marking fish and not catching them, adjust the leader distance until you find the sweet spot. If you do that and you still can't get a bite, then try switching to a different bait, something smaller, or bigger, or to a worm instead of a shad.

Choosing your bait is the next step. I typically use three baits when I'm drop-shotting smallmouth. I use a 3-inch Berkley Gulp Fry (green pumpkin), an Erie Darter by Poor Boys Baits (Golby), or a Zoom Super Fluke (white). I've had the most success on the Fry, it catches tons of fish and I have a lot of confidence in that bait. The Erie Darter has been pretty good to me whenever I've fished lakes that have been infested with gobies and I like to soak them in Goby Oil. The Super Fluke is the reason why I recommend the bigger Trokar hook. The hook doesn't bother the fish when using the smaller baits, and you'll need it for the fluke, and this is a big fish bait. I normally only throw this after I've caught a bunch of fish and I'm ready to go after the big ones. Pay close attention to the fish you're reeling in, often they'll puke during the fight and they'll tell you what they're eating and you can quickly match the hatch.

Next it's time to choose your rod. For years this was done with light-action spinning rods, with light line. However, recent developments in technology regarding how the rods are constructed make them far more sensitive in heavier action than before, allowing you to use a stiffer rod without sacrificing any of the feel you would have gotten in the lighter model. Why is that significant? Because it changes the finesse game. When choosing my drop-shot rod I want something really long, like 7'-6" or longer, because the key is to have the most amount of bend that you can get in the rod. That's what allows you to fight the fish the best. For this reason, you need to choose a rod with a really sensitive, fast tip. But I want my rods to have backbone, because I don't want to spend twenty minutes fighting a trophy fish on a light action rod. Now every time I talk to a large group of people and I start by telling them that this is my rod of choice, immediately there are numerous hands that go up from people who have heard for years that you need to use a light or medium-light rod. The story I always tell is of my friend Tyler Meadows who, after fishing Smith Mountain Lake in Virginia his entire life, came to fish with me at Oneida Lake in New York and insisted that a medium-light action rod was the key rod for a drop shot. Tyler hooked his first good smallmouth, and after about ten seconds he looked at me and said "Man, I can't turn this fish."

Lake Champlain skyline. Jon Fuchs

That lighter tackle will force you to wear those fish down to a point that is unhealthy for them. Using my setup allows me to feel the fish and set the hook, but to also have plenty of backbone in the rod that will in turn permit me to have some say in how things are going to go down. You might even say that you can "horse" those smaller fish a little bit with these newer rods.

When you choose your weight you'll want to pay close attention to these three factors: is there current and how much? Are there waves and how high? And what depth are you fishing? Here's a small breakdown for you:

¼ oz.	No Current	No Waves	under 20 Feet
½ oz.	Slight current	Waves less than 2 feet	20–30 feet
¾ oz.	2–5 mph drift	Waves over 3 feet	20–55 feet

The reason for this need to increase weight is because you want that sinker to be in contact with the bottom at all times. You don't want to cast your rig way out, just cast it enough so that you'll be fishing vertically from the boat. Pay attention to your electronics. When presenting the bait, don't shake the rod violently from one side to the other. What many people don't know is that even small ponds have some current, and larger bodies of water have lots of current. These baits react to that current and do all the moving for you. If you shake the bait too much, you'll actually make fish miss it. So keep your rod motionless and perpendicular to the water, and keep your line tight. Most of the time, you'll feel a tiny "tick" and your rod will get heavy, it might even feel like something is pulling it down, other times you'll get hit hard and it'll feel like the rod being ripped out of your hand. In either case, you don't need to set the hook like you do when you're flipping for largemouth. Just lift up the rod in a short, quick snap of the hand. Because the hook is pointed up, you'll have hooked that fish in the top of the mouth, which is right where you want to hook them, and you'll be able to start reeling them in. Don't be surprised if the fish seem small in the beginning. Many times the fight won't start until they see the boat, so be sure that your drag is set to allow them to make a run. Bigger fish will dive straight to the bottom, and fast. The best thing to do in this situation is hold the rod up, let them pull the line and don't try to reel. Once they reach the bottom you can start pulling them back up. If they try to jump, and they will, try to keep them from doing that by driving the rod into the water. Sometimes I'll shove half the rod underwater to keep them from coming out.

Gear

7'-6" medium graphite rod, or 7'-6" medium-heavy carbon fiber rod

2500 series spinning reel

12 lb KIMURA Jim Root Fishing Tournament Grade Fluorocarbon

Trokar Helix DS hooks

Bait: Strike King Dreamshot, Berkley Gulp nightcrawler

½ oz. or ¾ oz. Elite Tungsten Drop Shot weight

Weather

Spring and Fall: Not recommended other than to target spawning fish guarding beds in water more than 10 feet deep.

Summer: Hot and humid, best used to target fish in deep water. Windy days are great, but is also effective when calm.

Winter: Also a great tactic for deep holes.

There are a few other things you can do when you're in search mode. Sometimes I'll rig up two drop-shot hooks on the same line. I might put one at 3 feet, another at 18 inches, and then replace my drop shot weight with either a jig or a tube. This allows me to cover a lot of area in the water column, but it also allows me to use multiple baits at once. A tube, an Erie Darter, and a Super Fluke will tell you what type of food the fish are actively keying on, but will also lead to a bite from a finicky fish that was looking for something different. You won't get a lot of bites on the Super Fluke, but the ones you get will be good ones. I'll use this bait

Lake Erie drop shot smallmouth in mid fight.

in any weather condition, but it's especially effective during the summer and winter when the fish are deep. It will get bites from fish when the water is calm and the sun is bright, but it works best for me when there's a little wind because it will move the bait more, as long as you can keep the weight on the bottom.

14

Shaky Head

Another common type of finesse presentation is the shaky head. The shaky head is a great way to target smallmouth in any condition, and in any depth, during any time of year. I've caught fish on it shallow, deep, cold, hot. The biggest reason why this is so deadly is because it's very small and compact, and you're basically taunting the fish, daring them to bite. Now your rod setup can be very similar to your drop-shot setup in terms of action and weight of the rod, but I will always use at least a 7'-3" rod because I am casting and there are times

While it's possible to throw a shaky head on a casting rod, it's best done with a good spinning setup.
Russ Scalf

when I'll want to be able to get as much distance as I can, and will need a longer rod to make that happen. The Envy Series has a 7'-3" medium with incredible action, but don't be afraid to go with a rod that's 7'-6" or even 7'-9."

With line you can do it a couple different ways, and I will usually have two rods set up with each. If I'm fishing deep, clear lakes I use straight 10 lb fluorocarbon. But if I'm fishing shallow, or in rivers, I'll use braid with a short five-foot leader of fluorocarbon, and rather than use a Uni-Knot I prefer to use a small black barrel swivel, connected with Palomar knots. The key for that is to start with the shaky head hook and the leader, and tie your first knot, then tie the other end of the leader to the swivel, then tie the entire leader line to the braid. This is because of how the Palomar knot is executed, and the necessity to go in that order to allow the tag ends to pass through cleanly. If you forget and tie the swivel to the braid first it's ok, just tie your leader to the swivel but pass the line end through the loop of the knot instead of the other end of the line like you normally would (that would require you to pass the entire rod through a small loop, not convenient at all). If you can't spare a second rod, you can always purchase extra spools for your reels, so you can swap them out quickly depending on where you are.

When you rig your Shakey Head you'll want to use a finesse-type bait, like the Fry I mentioned earlier, and rig it nose down on a shaky-head hook like The Closer from Custom Cast. This way the worm is presented with the tail in the air, waving slightly like a hand in

The Closer Shakey Head jig by Custom Cast is a custom designed hook and head that always delivers maximum penetration.

a parade. To rig it you'll take the nose end and screw it on the hook, and softly put the sharp end of the hook into the worm where it lines up so the bait is straight. This hook will always land upright, so the bait will be presented exactly how you want it to be every single time. You'll want to work the bait in a couple different ways to see how the fish want it from one day to the next. Sometimes you'll have to just leave it alone for long periods of time, and work it real slow just by dragging it across the bottom. Other times you can bounce it off the bottom and work it back to you quicker in a hopping motion, or simply shake the rod back and forth in short fast wiggles. This bait is dynamite on shoals, main lake and secondary points, rocky shorelines, ledges, and in skinny grass. Don't hesitate to use larger worms. We tend to think that finesse fishing has to be done with little baits, but bigger fish often want bigger food, and there are finesse worms like the Fry that come in much bigger profiles. I've used a 12-inch ribbontail worm before and caught plenty of fish on it.

You should also open your mind to other possibilities with the shaky head hook. I've used it to rig small tubes, 3-inch swimbaits, plastic craws and beavers, goby imitations, and one of my favorite baits to throw on it is a Jackall Cross Tail Shad. That bait on a shaky head will look just like a feeding minnow or baby bass and can create a feeding frenzy! All of those baits will be worked the same way that I described before, but can allow you to target the fish in different ways with the right kind of forage that they're looking for. The hook is so versatile that there are very few limitations to what you're able to put on it.

The primary time for this bait is summer, especially when it's really hot, and there's little-to-no wind. Whenever those fish are pinned down and hard to get to bite, this really does show them something that's hard to resist that isn't a huge meal. So even if they're not hungry at the moment, you can get them to eat it just to get the bait to stop dancing in front of their face. Don't forget that smallmouth are predator fish, and they can be taunted into attacking something out of rage just as easily as they can out of hunger. This is a common theme throughout this book, and the biggest reason why you really need to use multiple presentations for each bait, so that you can engage each individual fish in the way that they need to in order to commit to your lure.

In fall the best place to use a shaky head is on ledges or islands. Cast into the shallowest part, and drag it off. Smallmouth will be cruising the shallow, suspended on the break, or on the bottom, and you can get them in all levels by just casting and dragging. The bait falls

The author and Johnny with some big Susky Smallies! Matt Dolinsky

slowly too, depending on how heavy your soft plastic lure and hook are. Rig the bait with a minnow-style bait, or 6-inch worm with a curly tail, green pumpkin or pink. An aggressive presentation works best.

This bait is just as good in the winter to target fish that are only eating smaller meals and when targeting fish that are guarding beds in the spring because you can drop it right in the bed and then shake it a lot to agitate fish that are already aggressively guarding eggs. This just goes to show how versatile this bait is, and why it's important to learn how to use it. What's really ironic though is that this is one of the easiest presentations to master, yet one of the most under-utilized. In fact, when I teach clinics to kids this is one of the first things I teach them to do because I learned by watching my good friend Ron use it to teach his son Trent. Using a shaky head is easy to do and catches giant fish, so clearly everyone should be doing it.

Gear:

7'-3" medium, fast-action casting rod; reel 7.1:1 or higher; 12 lb fluorocarbon line

7'-9" medium, fast-action spinning rod; 2500 series reel; KIMURA Jim Root Fishing 26 lb braid; 12 lb KIMURA Jim Root Fishing Tournament Grade Fluorocarbon leader; The Closer Shakey Head hook

Weather:

Spring: Deadly on bedding bass

Summer: Best used on calm, hot days on finicky fish, but a great choice on windy days to make long casts in deep water or on rocky points

Fall: Drag off of ledges to target suspended fish on windy days

Winter: Great way to target fish that are deep on the bottom and only eating tiny meals

15

Crayfish

Smallmouth will feast on shad during certain times of the year, but they are also incredibly fond of crayfish. At Oneida, in particular, there are areas that are covered with rocks that I refer to as big brown bowling balls. These rocks are a magnet for smallmouth bass, and I've caught smallmouth over 4 pounds in these areas and as shallow as 6–8 inches during the late spring/early summer during post spawn and again during the early fall feeding frenzy, because these rocks hold large numbers of crayfish. This particular food source is great for smallmouth because it's high in protein, and is fairly easy for the fish to digest. Luckily for you, this is also one of the easiest patterns to match!

How is that? Well, often smallmouth will puke while they're fighting on the other end of the line, or when they're in the livewell. When this happens you'll be able to see pieces of what they've been eating. When they're actively feeding on crayfish you'll be able to see lots of little claws, if not entire crayfish, floating or in the bottom of your livewell. This will not only tell you that you should be throwing jigs, tubes, or soft plastic craws, but it can even tell you what color to throw. During different stages of their life cycle, crayfish will change colors, and the closer you're able to match your bait to what the fish are eating, the more likely it is that they're going to eat it. And sometimes those small nuances are the difference between catching a hundred fish and catching zero. The fish are that picky. Unlike you and I, crayfish don't see one blue crayfish in a world full of orange crayfish as a delicious break from the norm. If all you have is blue, it's better than nothing, and you might be able to get a few, but you really need to try to find out as much as you can about the species in each body of water, as they can be very different. Most people who guide for smallmouth use crayfish as their primary bait during trips with clients because they're cheaper than buying soft plastic baits and hard lures, they require no real fishing prowess to use, and they're incredibly effective. But you can be sure those guides know what color crayfish to use.

Exactly how much can crayfish differ from one another? Well there are some lakes in the Northeast, Oneida being one of them, that have a rare species of blue-green crayfish.

Smallmouth feed heavily on crayfish and will eat them as often as they can. Russ Scalf

There are other lakes near Oneida that also have that same sub-species, including Ontario. Information like this is one of the many keys to catching giant smallmouth. I found this bit of information after scouring the Internet for hours and finding an obscure research project that was done by a professor at Cornell University. But another great way to learn about the crayfish in a particular lake is to just buy a trap, fill it with some bread, put it in the water, leave it out overnight and catch some. This will help you tremendously and is a nominal investment for the knowledge you'll receive. Full and new moons are particularly great times to target smallmouth with crayfish or baits that imitate them, as this can be a time when crayfish are shedding their shells due to growth, and the bass will target them heavily. When it comes to mimicking crayfish, you have three options: tubes, jigs, and craws. I'll break down each of them next.

Gear:

7' medium, fast-action spinning rod; 2500 series reel; 15 lb KIMURA Jim Root Fishing Fluorocarbon line; Trokar TK100 3/0 hook.

The author caught this fish right after the fish in the previous picture on the same exact tube. Tubes are much more durable than other plastic baits and can hold up over multiple catches. Russ Scalf

Weather:

Live crayfish can be used all year, in all conditions. This is the primary bait used by most smallmouth guides in the Northeast as it is a favorite forage for smallmouth.

TUBES

One of my favorite ways to target smallmouth is with a tube, and without a doubt it's produced some of my biggest smallmouth. Tubes are also incredibly durable; unlike a traditional soft plastic worm that might only sustain one or two fish before tearing apart, you can catch many on a tube and have it look just like it did when you rigged it. Tubes are designed to mimic crayfish and can be fished slowly by dragging them on the bottom, or faster in a "hopping" motion. Where you are and what type of water you're fishing will determine your presentation and setup. There are a few different ways that I rig tubes: Texas, Mendota, open, and brass hook tube jig. Each is unique and designed for a specific location.

Let's start with the rod choice. When I'm smallmouth bass fishing with tubes I either use a 7' medium, fast-action casting rod with a high-speed reel at least 7 or higher (I use an 8:1.1) or I'll use a 7' to 7'-6" spinning rod, medium, fast-action with a 2500 size reel. My casting rod is spooled up with 50 lb braid with a 20 lb leader, and my spinning rod will have 10–15 lb fluorocarbon line. When I'm fishing in rivers I tend to use the spinning rig because I am moving a lot, making short/tight casts, and I want the bait to sink quickly in the current. When I'm fishing lakes where I'm either targeting submerged vegetation or shoals I want the extra backbone to lift fish out of those weeds in the deeper depths, which is why I'll use the casting rod.

I fish Oneida Lake probably the most of any body of water in New York, and when I'm there I'm usually in 8–15 feet of water, fishing grass lines and submerged vegetation. If the grass is really thick, I'll use a Mendota Rig or Texas rig my tube. If I am using a Texas rig, I will use a Trokar 4/0 TK120, a ½ oz. Elite Tungsten Black flipping weight (pegged). These presentations will allow me to stay weedless. However, because tubes are often made with thicker plastic (particularly the magnum size that I fish most often), Texas rigging can lead to missing a lot of fish due to the way smallmouth bass eat. I want to fish my tubes with an exposed hook, and I set the hook the second that I feel a bite on the line to reduce the number of missed opportunities. For this I'll use the Trokar tube hook TK190 4/0. If my tube is a little small for that I'll downsize until I am able to find the hook that bends where the skirt begins on the tube. When it comes to how I fish it, that will depend on whether I'm fishing grass lines or deeper. If I'm pitching at grass I work fast. Pitch the bait and let it fall, wait a couple seconds and pop it once, wait a couple seconds and pull it out, and try again on a different piece of that grass. Smallmouth can position themselves so that they won't see your bait unless you present it from a certain angle, so you have to work those isolated patches of grass from all sides. When I'm fishing deeper I'll present it differently depending on if I can see them on my graph suspended or on the bottom, and I'll usually make multiple passes over an area that I know holds fish so that I can give them the opportunities to see it differently. The first time through an area I work really fast. I start with a long cast, I count down the bait to the approximate depth I'm targeting, and then I start snapping the rod up and down constantly and in erratic patterns. (If you watched me from the side it would look like I was quickly raising and lowering my rod from 7 o'clock to 10 or 11.) After I canvas that area I'll turn around, and do the same thing from the other direction. If that hasn't produced any fish I'll go back over my original drift and work slower, dragging the tube on the bottom. You will lose a fair amount of baits this way, but dragging them on the bottom can be a very productive way to present your tube.

Which is exactly what you'll do in the rivers, but with a different setup. Because river smallmouth are not like lake fish, I use a smaller tube, with a lead tube jig that's got a brass hook. The reason for this is because rivers are notorious for having debris and/or rocks on the bottom that will snag your line again and again and again. Not only do I not want to lose a ton of hooks, but having to retie in moving current is really not fun at all. The brass hook will bend, so 99 percent of the time I can retrieve it from any snag by pulling hard enough to bend the hook, and then I'll rebend the hook once I get it back in the boat. To tie this, you really have to put the tube on the hook first and poke the eye through the side of the tube. When your tube needs to be

The author prefers the magnum size tube because it catches bigger fish than the smaller tubes.

replaced you'll have to cut the line. I've tried passing tubes over the lead head, but it stretches the tube too much so I won't do it. What I'll do is rig up three rods with tubes so I can grab another quickly and retie when it's convenient, and I'll also prep a bunch of heads and tubes so that the bait is already on the hook, and all I have to do is tie a quick Palomar knot and I'm ready to go! When presenting the bait I want it on the bottom, and I just bounce it a little bit. Usually a ¼ oz. jig head is more than enough for shallow water (10 feet or less), and I really wouldn't use much bigger than a ½ oz.

Gear:

7'-3" medium-heavy fast-action casting rod; high-speed reel 7.1:1 or higher; 12 lb KIMURA Jim Root Fishing Tournament Grade Fluorocarbon line; Trokar TK190 hook; Elite Tungsten ½ oz. bullet weight; Bass Pro Shops magnum flipping tube

7'-9" medium, fast-action spinning rod; 2500 series reel; KIMURA Jim Root Fishing 26 lb braid; 12 lb KIMURA Jim Root Fishing Tournament Grade Fluorocarbon leader; brass-weighted ⅜ oz. tube hook

Weather:

Spring: Sunny, clear water, water temp 50°F–60°F

Summer: Sunny, windy, clear water, water temp 70°F and up

Fall: Shallow, clear water, any temp

Winter: Deep, slow moving water, water temp 42°F and below

PLASTIC CRAWS

This is a bait that's gotten very popular over the past five years because of the advancements in the fishing industry. Bait companies are making soft plastic crayfish that look exactly like what you find in the water. The shape, the small details in the curves of the body, and the softness of the plastic make this bait an incredible tool and a must-have in any smallmouth angler's tackle box. There are many different ways you can present these baits, and all of them catch fish during different times of the year.

My favorite soft plastic crayfish is made by Whip 'Em Baits and is pictured below. I like this bait because the size, the texture, and the color combinations of green/orange and blue/green have produced giant fish for me. Also, it doesn't have an overpowering scent, which I have found smallmouth prefer. I fish this in the 6–12 foot range and flip it around areas of submerged vegetation. My rod is a 7' medium action, paired with a high-speed reel, spooled with 15 lb fluorocarbon line. I use an Elite Tungsten ¼–⅜ oz. weight, depending on how deep I'm fishing. I peg the weight to keep it from sliding and I use a Trokar hook (TK120) that's a little wider than other soft plastics I use because I want that wider gap to help get the bait out of the way when I'm setting the hook. You'll want to rig the bait Texas so it's weedless, with the claws pointing away from the knot as shown below. This is also meant to look as realistic as possible, as crayfish move in reverse when they're moving quickly.

The Whip 'Em Baits 4" Torpedo Craw is by far the author's favorite. It's a hollow body craw, and this Alabama Craw color is incredible.

I look for isolated patches of grass in and along drop-offs or on weedlines. I work this bait quickly by pitching it around the patch of grass in front of me, I pause for about three seconds once it's landed on the bottom before I jerk the rod in a short quick motion to give the bait a small hop, let it rest again for a couple seconds, then if I haven't gotten a bite I'll put it out and try the other side of the grass. Sometimes the fish are positioned in a certain way that requires you to show them the bait from a particular angle to get them to eat it. Practice your flips. You want the bait to enter the water like an Olympic diver, with as little splash and noise as possible. This is achieved by having your reel properly tuned and by making short flips and pitches rather than trying to cast long distances. Small distances of 8–10 feet are more than enough to engage hungry fish, while allowing you to reach out with minimal force to propel your bait. Chapter 11, "Texas Rigs," has further detail about how to rig this bait and work it.

Gear:

7'-3" medium-heavy fast-action casting rod; high-speed reel 7.1:1 or higher; 12 lb Jim Root Fishing Fluorocarbon line; Trokar TK130 3/0 hook; Elite Tungsten ½ oz. bullet weight; Bass Pro Shops magnum flipping tube

7'-9" medium, fast-action spinning rod; 2500 series reel; KIMURA Jim Root Fishing 35 lb braid; 12 lb KIMURA Jim Root Fishing Tournament Grade Fluorocarbon leader; brass-weighted ⅜ oz. tube hook

Weather:

Spring: Sunny, clear water, water temp 50°F–60°F

Summer: Sunny, windy, water temp 75°F and up

Fall: Shallow, clear water, any temp

Winter: Deep, slow moving water, water temp 42°F and below

16

Jigs

The jig is a big fish bait that can be used all year, in all seasons, in all conditions. Depending on the time of year and the depth I'm fishing, I may use one as small as a ¼ oz., or as big as 1¼ oz. A jig is basically a hook with a weighted head that comes in roughly three shapes: standard, swim, or football, with a skirt attached. Standard jigs and football-head jigs are both fished relatively the same (on the bottom) while swim jigs are retrieved to mimic a swimming fish, and are therefore reeled in like you would a spinnerbait or crankbait. I have never had much success with swim jigs when targeting smallmouth, so this passage will focus on the other two types, which you'll use pretty much the same. There are also some instances that I'll mention later on when I use a football head without the weed guard and without the skirt. This is a special application used to target deep smallmouth in the Great Lakes.

When it comes to jigs you're still imitating a crayfish. The difference is the skirt and the long weed guard that protrudes out and over the tip of the hook. Many jigs also feature a corkscrew where the hook meets the weighted head to hold the piece of soft plastic that you'll use to complete the setup of this bait. On jigs that are ½ oz. and up, I use the same craw that I described above. If I'm using a smaller jig, like a Little D,

Custom Cast Little D is the perfect smallmouth jig because it's heavy enough to get down, but it has a very compact, low profile design that resembles a small meal, making it hard to resist.

then I'll use something smaller like a paca-chunk that has a smaller body, but the claws are the same size. Because the craws I use (and the ones like them) are hollow, you're not able to just cut the body in half and attach it to the hook the same way, so you really need a smaller profile bait for smaller jigs. You don't have to use craws—you can use beavers or creature baits—but I prefer them to look as lifelike as possible.

I use jigs on a 7'-6" medium-heavy rod or a 7'-11" heavy rod with fast-action tips and high-speed casting reels. I use 15 lb fluorocarbon line, and I cast these jigs far and drag them on the bottom. I use them in areas where there are a lot of transition periods in lakes, like shoals and sunken islands, or in rivers where there's a lot of current and a nice rocky bottom. What kind of jig you use is up to you, and there are lots to choose from. There are only two points that I stress; the first is that it's to your advantage to use one that is made with a Trokar hook, because often there is a lot of space between you and the bait, and you want to be sure you get a real good hook set on that fish. The second is that it's okay to trim the weed guard back a little. This will increase your hook rate, and you'll still have plenty of protection from weeds, especially in the areas where you're going to be using these jigs.

Once you've casted it, you just want to drag it on the bottom. After each cast, run your fingers down the last two or three feet of line so you can make sure there are no abrasions from rocks, zebra mussels, or other sharp objects on the floor of the water. If you find any

Mille Lacs smallmouth caught on the Custom Cast Little D, Jack's Craw color.

rough spots or irregularities, cut the jig, remove the bad spot, and retie. Large smallmouth can break even the toughest line; any damage, no matter how small it may seem, can be exploited when fighting these fish, and the last thing you'll want to see is that fish of a lifetime falling slowly out of sight with your lure in their mouth.

I also want to point out that in chapter 13 I talked about the drop shot and the special weight that's used on the bottom. When I'm targeting fish that I've marked on the bottom and using a drop shot I'll often use a jig or a tube on the bottom instead of the drop shot weight. This will tell me what the fish prefer to eat: shad, crayfish, etc. If I'm hitting on the drop shot over and over, I'll just keep with it. But if they are hitting the jig, I'll use my jig rod and put the drop shot rod away because it will have more backbone when it comes to fighting those fish.

Gear:

7'-3" medium-heavy fast-action casting rod; high-speed reel 7.1:1 or higher; 12 lb Jim Root Fishing Fluorocarbon line; Custom Cast Little D Jig; Whip 'Em Baits Torpedo craw

Weather:

Spring: Sunny, clear water, water temp 50°F–60°F

Summer: Sunny, windy, clear deep water, water temp 70°F and up

Fall: Shallow, windy, any temp

Winter: Deep, slow moving water, water temp 42°F and below

17

Swimbaits

This is, by far, the best way to catch a giant smallmouth. There's something that is a part of the smallmouth DNA that programs them to be unable to resist a swimbait if presented properly. The problem is that most people don't understand that, can't learn it, become frustrated by it, and give up. The first time I threw a swimbait I watched my buddy Matty outfish me 35–1. We were in the same boat, using the same bait, and I could've sworn I was doing the same thing. By the end of the day I was beyond frustrated, but I stayed with it until I figured out the proper cadence, angle, and was able to master the presentation to the point that the table would be reversed some days and I would out-fish him like I did at Ontario when I bagged almost thirty pounds and he caught zero. I now have gotten so comfortable with this bait that it is my number one method of targeting smallmouth bass all year. And it's the only setup that I will take with me every day, regardless of where I'm going, or the time of the year.

When I started using a swimbait I was throwing a small 3-inch bait on a jig head with a spinning rod and 12 lb fluorocarbon. Now to be fair, there are lots of people who still use that setup and you can catch them with it. But I switched to a casting rod during an Erie trip and I strongly advise you to do the same. I've spent probably close to a thousand hours on the water throwing this bait, and have caught over five thousand smallmouth on swimbaits, and have found the absolute perfect rod, reel, and bait. The rod is an Omen Black Series cranking rod called "Crankenstein" by 13 Fishing, and I use either a 6.6:1 or 6.3:1 Concept A casting reel spooled with 12 lb Jim Root Fishing Tournament Grade Fluorocarbon line. The hooks that I use are ones that I make myself with a Trokar hook and a unique head that I have custom poured, but you can use any simple jig head to learn. I tend to like one with a large head, as this will increase the roll of the bait during the retrieve. You should probably use a little drop of Superglue on the jig head to keep the swimbaits in place, and make them up the night before if you can. The only downside to rubber swimbaits is that the fish will tear them up quickly. My preference for swimbaits is the Reaction Innovation Sungill.

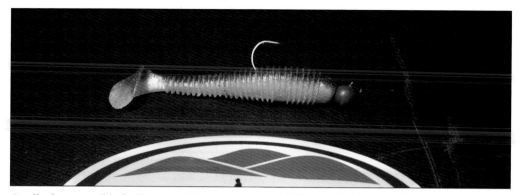

Small adjustments like hook size/weight can make all the difference. Anthony Lorefice

Don't be fooled by other swimbaits that cost more money; this is by far the best soft plastic swimbait on the market, and the fish can't resist it. When you're fishing in rivers or on a lake when there's little or no wind, you should start with a lighter-weight jig head. If there's a lot of current or wind, or if you're fishing deeper areas with a 5-inch bait then I recommend using at least a ½ oz. jig head. I know there are a lot of weighted belly, weedless swimbait hooks on the market right now, but you'll miss a lot of fish with those, and there's no gain by having a weedless hook. The exposed hook of the standard jig head will rarely, if ever, collect weeds. And your hookup ratio with the exposed hook will be so much higher.

Setting up the rod and baits are easy, but learning the cadence and presentation can be really difficult. If you reel the bait too fast the fish won't eat it. You want to reel it just fast enough to make the tail wag back and forth. When choosing your rod, make sure that it's sensitive enough that you can feel that movement in the tail while you learn. The thing that makes this bait so deadly is that it needs to look like a big dumb meal that just made a huge mistake. Seeing a small fish slowly lumbering by goes against every shred of programming that fish are born with, which is why they have to eat it. Not only that, but the fact that they're silent baits means that they won't spook fish that have been pressured by other anglers the way that crankbaits and other noise-producing baits will. So what is it about this presentation that makes it so difficult?

It really is all about the speed. The rate that you retrieve a swimbait has to be precise and it's influenced by so many things. Wind and current can change quickly, so you need to establish a level of comfort with this bait to be able to make these tiny adjustments. Like I said before about the first time I threw it with Matty, I could've sworn I was reeling it the exact same way that he was but I wasn't getting any bites. Part of the problem was that I wasn't reeling it in at the same speed even though I thought I was, and the other part was the angle that he was retrieving the bait was different, which also contributed to the rate of speed

Lake Ontario giant smallmouth, at one time the author's personal best.

the bait was coming back to the boat. This was mentioned in part previously when I talked about finding the hive. Presentation with this bait is paramount to your success. If you think you're reeling slowly, slow down because you probably aren't reeling slowly enough.

When I'm really catching a lot of fish on a swimbait it's exciting, and I'll realize that I'm reeling too fast and need to remind myself to slow down occasionally. Because I've thrown it so much I can usually tell what speed I should be bringing it in, and I'll sing different songs

Megabass Magdraft Swimbaits are great smallmouth baits!

to myself that have beat patterns that match the particular cadence that is working for that day. This helps to keep me focused on what I'm doing, and keeps the bait in the hive regularly. When I'm at the lake I also need to remember the angle that I'm retrieving my bait, so that it stays at the same speed while I drift. In rivers, this is even more of an issue because I'm targeting fish that are relating to shoreline drop-offs or points and the strikes should come within the first ten feet of the shore and the current plays such a huge part. So whenever possible try to land your bait as close to the edge as you can and bring it downstream with the current. Smallmouth face upstream, and this will allow the bait to be in their face for the longest period of time.

When they bite this bait, you'll feel a small "tick" on your line. Set the hook by lifting the rod up. This will help you try to set the hook in the upper part of the fish's mouth, which will make it virtually impossible for the fish to shake off. After you set the hook, if the fish isn't hooked, slow down and let the bait fall. Smallmouth will often ram a bait in an attempt to stun it, and will come back after in full attack to eat it. I've even seen them do this three or four times on one retrieve, so don't fret if the fish bites but isn't there. Ninety-nine percent

Megabass Swimbait. B. C. Forester

of the time they'll come back and hit it again. If they don't hit it again, cast right back in the same place. Once they do hit and you've set the hook, immediately point your rod tip down and reel that fish in as fast as you can. I've even been known to bury the tip of my rod as far into the water as I can to try to prevent the fish from jumping. The ideal weather pattern for this technique is cloudy/partly cloudy and windy (5–8 mph), or in water that is slightly stained. If the water is too clear the fish will see you, and you'll need to make extremely long casts to succeed.

The big swimbaits are a different breed altogether, and take a lot of confidence to throw. I don't recommend starting with a 9-inch swimbait because they are incredibly expensive and you will probably not do it right. If you don't work the bait properly the fish won't eat it. Starting out on a smaller 5-inch bait is absolutely the way to go, and you can move up as your confidence increases. My personal favorites are Megabass Magslowl because they are just the right size for giant smallmouth, and the tail action is perfectly irresistible. You have to remember that when you throw this bait, you're often fishing all day long for one bite. This can get very frustrating when you're watching other people catch one after another. You have to remind yourself that they aren't going to catch the size of the fish that you are, and to stay the course. Try to be encouraged by what you're seeing. Tell yourself that it's good that they're catching them because it proves you're around fish, and often catching them can help to fire up the school and get other nearby fish to bite.

Lastly, I want to say that below in my list of weather conditions you'll see the best weather patterns for each season, but this is the one bait that I throw all year long. I never go smallmouth fishing without a swimbait. I use it in the Delaware River, Oneida Lake, Erie, everyplace I have ever fished for smallmouth I've used a swimbait. I strongly encourage you invest the time to learn.

Gear:

7'-6" medium, fast-action casting rod; 6.3:1 for lakes 6.6:1 for rivers; 12 lb KIMURA Jim Root Fishing Fluorocarbon line; swimbait hook in either ¼ or ½ oz.

7'-9" heavy, fast-action rod; 5.3:1 reel; KIMURA Jim Root Fishing 26 lb braid for backing; 20 lb Jim Root Fishing Tournament Grade Fluorocarbon line (giant swimbait setup)

Weather:

Spring: Cloudy, clear water, water temp 48°F–60°F

Summer: Cloudy, windy, clear water, water temp 70°F and up

Fall: Shallow, clear water, any temp

Winter: Deep, slow moving water, water temp 42°F and below

THE DONKEY KONG RIG

The other way to use the swimbait is on a Donkey Kong Rig, which was invented by my friend Larry Mazur who was looking for a way to target smallmouth that were feeding on gobies. Unlike the previously-mentioned tactic for swimbaits, this one is a bit more complex and really requires some high-end electronics to properly execute. To set up the Donkey Kong Rig (DKR) you'll want to start with a ¾ oz. football-head jig without a skirt that you rig to your 5- to 7-inch swimbait. Hook the swimbait the same way you did the jig head with the hook exposed out the top of the bait. Rig this up on a jig rod. Mine is an 8' rod, medium-weight, fast-action, because I want as much length as I can get fishing this deep and with this much line out. I use a high-speed reel with a gear ratio of 8 or higher, spooled with 12 lb fluorocarbon line as a 5' leader only, with the rest of the line being 50 lb braid. Be sure you tie a good knot when you connect your lines, and that you haven't made any line stretching in the process. Tying fluoro to braid can be one of the most difficult things to do, but if you use a Double Albrecht knot you should be able to accomplish this. If you need assistance with the knot you can watch the video on it in the gear section.

Lake Erie smallmouth. Jon Fuchs

The reason why you'll want a stiffer rod is because of the way that you're going to be presenting this bait, and where you're going to be targeting the fish. You'll mainly be focusing on areas in the lake that have sand bottoms. How do you know the bottom is sand? To begin with you need good electronics. I've used Humminbird my entire life, and as I'm writing this I'm using the new Helix 12s. In my opinion these units offer the best look at an updated Navionics card, and try to find areas that look like they have nothing there; no shoals or sunken islands, no steep drop-offs. Go there and switch your screen to the 3-D sonar and view in sidescan mode, and if you've correctly found areas with sandy bottoms you'll actually see what looks like waves on the bottom. That's because you're looking at waves of sand, similar to what you'd see on the beach. You'll want to drift across areas like this, so you'll need some wind to help push you.

Cast your bait out to the side of the boat as far as you can, and let it fall to the bottom. Make sure you have enough line out so that your bait is roughly fifty yards out behind the boat and on the bottom. Go back to your graph and switch to 2-D downscan view and zoom in so you see only the bottom five feet. You're looking to see little red bumps on the bottom, which is a smallmouth that's buried itself down in the sand a little bit. That's why you need to zoom in so far. If you just drifted over that spot in the regular view you would never see that fish. Once you pass those spots you can count down five to ten seconds and you should feel the "tick" of the smallmouth hitting your bait. Set the hook immediately and try not to waste your time getting that fish in the boat. Being that these fish are typically pretty deep (over twenty feet) you'll want to be sure to return them to the water quickly so that you don't have to fizz them. If you're keeping them momentarily with plans to release them later you'll have to fizz these fish or apply fin weights to keep them down and upright in your livewells.

I also want to point out that this technique that Larry found goes against everything you ever thought you knew about smallmouth bass. Smallmouth in sand is an adaptation to the species in response to the goby infestation, and there are sure to be new ways to target them as we continue to learn more about the goby and the ways they impact our waters. Ideal weather for this pattern is cloudy, windy (5–8 mph), falling or steady barometric pressure. The key is the wind, without it you won't be able to drift properly and if there's too much you won't be able to keep your bait on the bottom and there's an added risk of waves that create dangerous water. It's good to keep a drift sock in your boat in case the wind is too strong to drift properly, but not so strong that there's a small-craft advisory on the lake. Attach this to the rear of the boat, let it sink, and slowly let it out behind you. This should help you stay at the ideal drifting speed of approximately 1.5 mph. A word to the wise: don't use a drift sock if there's current where you're fishing or it will have the opposite effect and will speed you up rather than slow you down.

Gear:

7'-6" medium-heavy, fast-action casting rod; high-speed reel 7.3:1 or higher; 12 lb KIMURA Jim Root Fishing Fluorocarbon line; swimbait hook in either ¼, ½, or ¾ oz.

Weather:

Spring: Cloudy, clear water, water temp 50°F–55°F

Summer: Cloudy, windy, clear water, water temp 70°F and up

Fall: Shallow, clear water, any temp

Winter: Deep, slow moving water, water temp 42°F and below

18

Spinnerbaits

When I began thinking about how I was going to write this chapter in the winter of 2015, my thought was that it would be introduced by a brief discussion around the fact that the art of throwing a spinnerbait was pretty much a forgotten practice nowadays. We have come so far in the development of new baits that many people, especially young anglers, don't appreciate the effectiveness of this bait. Then Jason Christie nearly won the 2016 Bassmaster Classic on a spinnerbait and gave new life to an old technique for chasing big bass. But the

Did you know that sometimes you can just pitch a spinnerbait like you do a jig? You don't always need to make a really long cast! Russ Scalf

truth is that it's one of the most deadly smallmouth bass fishing lures you can have if you know how to use it properly.

What's really great about spinnerbaits is their versatility. Spinnerbaits come in an enormous range of size/weight/color/blade combinations and understanding these differences is the first step in assembling the proper setup. For me it comes down to two baits that have some basic similarities, while being drastically different at the same time. The first is made by Strike King. It's a Tour Grade, in Sexy Shad color, with two blades that are referred to as "tandem." The first blade closest to the knot is a gold Colorado, and the second blade is a silver willow. The reason for this pairing is because they serve different functions. The willow blade reflects light in order to mimic baitfish, while the Colorado blade creates sound/vibration, and allows me to slow the bait down. I always use a trailer hook, and I usually don't put a swimbait on the spinnerbait. Normally when I'm using this spinnerbait, I'm in a deepwater lake like Oneida or Ontario, so the most important part is the size; I never use anything less than a ½ oz., and there are very good reasons for this.

I want this bait to look really big, because I want it to seem like a school of fish, not just one lonely minnow. Fish are so opportunistic that the higher the perceived success rate, the more likely the fish are to try to eat it. So when they look up and see what appears to be a school of baitfish, it's worth the effort more often than it is when they see just one or two. It is also very important that you be able to present the bait properly, and when you have wind that creates waves larger than one foot, you want that bait to sink a little bit while still being able to reel it at the proper speed. If you reel too slowly the blades won't spin, and the bait won't be attractive to the fish. The heavier spinnerbaits also tend to have larger blades, which will create more sound/vibration and reflect more light. This is my one of my favorite lures at Oneida, Ontario, and the St. Lawrence River all year round.

The other spinnerbait I use is a Randy Watson, Sexy Sinner. It's custom made for me by Randy Watson, and I have never shared this until now because I've wanted

Strike King Tour Grade (left), Randy Watson Sexy Sinner (right).

it to stay a secret because, honestly, it's that good. It's also a tandem rig, same color blades, slightly different design, with a unique profile of the spinnerbait. The color pattern is made to look like a wounded goby, and it's my favorite spinnerbait to use in current or on days when there is little or no wind. In any New York river that has smallmouth bass this bait is absolutely deadly when worked down shorelines or along current breaks.

I throw these baits on either my 7'-3" medium-action Omen Black, or my Crankenstein, with either a 6:3 (lake) or 6:6 (river) reel, with 10 lb fluorocarbon. In the lake I am just throwing it in a sweeping motion across the front of the boat whenever I come to a new area of the lake, or when I see fish busting on the surface and a topwater isn't an option (sunny days or days with extreme wind). It's also really great to throw in weed beds or on rocky points. With this bait one of the parts of presentation that is often overlooked is the way it can slap the water when casted if done properly, allowing it to sound just like a fish that has busted on the surface.

In rivers you'll still want to throw it anywhere, but you want to cast upstream and retrieve it down, and depending on how much current there is you may need to do it at an angle that will allow you to bring it slow enough to give the fish enough time to see it and react to it, but fast enough to turn the blades. The slightly smaller profile of the Randy Watson will give the bait more appeal to river fish because of the increased frequency with which these fish tend to eat when having to live in current all the time compared to their lake-living cousins

When you are making really long casts it's best to do it sidearm because it will reduce the amount of wind resistance you'll encounter during the cast and maximize your distance. Russ Scalf

Spinnerbaits are great for covering lots of water. Anthony Lorefice

who can take a giant meal and then go rest somewhere. Also, the likelihood of finding large schools of bait in rivers isn't as high as it is in lakes, and you want to present the fish with things they're accustomed to seeing when trying to entice them into feeding. In either situation, this bait should be on the deck at all times. Don't underestimate a smallmouth's ability to spit this lure. The trailer hook is essential and even with it they'll shake this bait in the air if you let them. Rod control is key, and you want to keep that fish from jumping as much as you can. This bait can be worked deep, shallow, and anywhere in between. You can burn it across the top, or drag it on the bottom. Anyplace where smallmouth feed on baitfish is a great place to use this lure.

When it comes to weather patterns, my favorite conditions for throwing this bait would be morning and night, or windy/overcast days, especially if there's a lot of wind and the fish are on a shad bite. I can cover a lot of water with this bait, and I can work it pretty quick through different depths to find what range the fish are best relating to. The spinnerbait is probably one of the best search baits ever created, so learn to use it because you can rely on it heavily when you travel to new bodies of water.

Gear:

7'-3" medium, fast-action casting rod; reel in 6.6:1 or 6.3:1; 12 lb KIMURA Jim Root Fishing Fluorocarbon line

Weather:

Spring: Partly sunny, clear/stained water, water temp 50°F–60°F, depth 7–10 feet

Summer: Cloudy, windy, clear water, water temp 70°F and up, depth 5–25 feet

Fall: Shallow, clear water, water temp 55°F–65°F

Winter: Warm days, slight wind, water temp 40°F–50°F, depth 8–12 feet

19

Double Fluke Rig

The Donkey Kong Rig or double fluke rig is something that not many people have heard of, but has quickly become one of the most successful ways to catch big smallmouth in rivers. I first learned about this technique while on a fishing trip in Harrisburg on the Susquehanna River near Three Mile Island. I'd used a single fluke to target largemouth, but had never heard of using it for smallmouth or using a double. When it's all set up you have a swivel that splits into two lines, one is roughly 18 inches long, and the other is roughly 28 inches long, so that the two baits are spaced apart from each other. To do this properly you want to tie an 18-inch leader on one end of a barrel swivel, and then you'll pass your line from your rod through the other end. Next you'll take that line from your rod and attach it to another barrel swivel. Finally you'll attach another leader to the open end of that swivel, this time you'll want it to be about 24 inches in length. You want to be sure to give yourself enough room to tie your hooks so that you'll have about 12 inches of line on the short leader and about 18 inches of line on the long leader.

When I rig this bait I use a Trokar TK100 3/0 hook tied with 12 lb Fluorocarbon. I love this hook for throwing a fluke because it's super sharp, but has the perfect design for a fluke because it tucks up nicely against the belly of the bait so

Trokar HD Worm Hooks are the author's favorite for flukes.

The author's buddy Matty with two double fluke rig smallies.

that it's completely hidden from the fish and it doesn't impede the action of the fluke at all. It's also a little heavy, so it will help your bait to sink just a little bit. For flukes, I use the Zoom Super Fluke, in either all white or white with a chartreuse tail. I prefer to throw them on a long, stiff rod because they're very light and I want to be able to make long casts but they're also going to be worked like drop shots and I want to be able to get that kind of action out of them during the retrieve. I have a jig rod that works perfectly for this with a high-speed reel that's spooled up with the same fluoro I use when jigging in clear water. When done properly, the tandem flukes will dart from side to side like synchronized swimmers, moving in unison from right to left. You'll want to do this slowly and carefully, and there's a very specific cadence that you need to use to be successful. Vary speeds until you find the right one. Pay close attention to what's going on under the surface when you're retrieving the bait. Many times nearby smallmouth will come and attempt to attack the second lure. Because it's moving so fast, they might miss it once or twice, but if you have decent rod control you can continue to bring in the hooked fish and give the chasing fish an opportunity to double your pleasure. I doubled many times during that trip and was impressed by the second fish's ability to catch the bait that was moving so quickly.

The best places to use this rig are in and around docks, along current breaks, and near rocky points. As you can see this is clearly a shallow-water bait, best used in under 12 feet of water. In any of the places the retrieve will be the same, roughly 3–6 feet below the surface, and with the same cadence. This is one of my favorite techniques for targeting smallmouth when there is little-to-no wind and sunny skies because, although you're working it like a drop shot, I still consider it a finesse bite, and the sun really seems to make this presentation more effective. It's also a great way to target fish that are highly pressured because it's silent and has very erratic movements.

The only difficult part of using this rig is the swivel at the top. Because you really don't want too big a swivel or it'll impact your action, but you don't want too small of one either. I also want to point out that while I have seen some people use a spinning rod for this rig, I don't recommend it because fighting one smallmouth on a spinning rod can be hard

Double flukes in the river can often produce double giants.

enough. Even if you do manage to get the fish in, you can severely damage the fish by having to tire them out to a point that is unhealthy for them, particularly if they live in current and don't have calm water where they can regain their strength.

Gear:

7'-6" medium, fast-action casting rod; reel 7.1:1 or higher; 10 lb KIMURA Jim Root Fishing Fluorocarbon line; Trokar TK100 3/0 hook

7'-6" medium-heavy, fast-action spinning rod; 2500 series reel; 10 lb KIMURA Jim Root Fishing Fluorocarbon line; Trokar TK100 3/0 hook

Weather:

Spring: Sunny, clear water, water temp 40°F–50°F, shallow

Summer: Sunny/mostly sunny, calm, clear water, water temp 70°F and up, depth 5–10 feet

Fall: Shallow, clear water, water temp 60°F and below

Winter: Great winter bait on calm days for rivers or shallow lakes at depths of less than 10 feet

20

Carolina Rigs

Many people already know that a Carolina rig is a great way to target largemouth bass because they'll always eat it, but what they probably don't know is that it's also a great tool for targeting deep smallmouth bass in summer and winter. What prevents people from doing it is an inability to get over the fact that they're in deep water. When you take someone out of their shallow-water element and tell them to do the same thing in water that's 15, 25, or even 35 feet deep, they have a momentary brain malfunction that shouldn't happen. That space between you and the bottom of the lake is a buffer zone, it's an advantage for you that you need to appreciate and run to, not from. Not only will smallmouth hit a Carolina rig that deep, they'll rip the rod out of your hand if you're not careful!

Does this mean you can only throw a Carolina rig in deep water? No, of course not. I've used it to target fish in as little as 7 feet with a fluke, tube, or swimbait. With that being said, it's one of my favorite techniques for targeting deep fish because I can use a giant bait like an 8-inch salamander or a Super Brush Hog that will trigger bites from bigger fish, but I can also use a smaller tube if the fish aren't willing to eat a big bait, and the weight will still get my bait down like I need it to. The rod you'll want to use is going to be something really long, at least 7'-6" medium-heavy, fast or extra fast-action, with at least 12 lb fluorocarbon line on a high-speed reel. I prefer a 7'-11" rod because it helps me make long casts and

A fully assembled Carolina rig.

I can catch up quickly when the fish are moving. The reason why you want the heavier line is because you're going to be dragging this bait across rocks and other sharp objects, and you don't want to lose a fish during the retrieve.

So how do you set up a Carolina rig? Well to start with you need the proper components: a barrel swivel, brass weights (I prefer to use ¼ oz. weights), glass beads, monofilament line, a hook, and a soft plastic bait. First you slide a weight onto the line. I prefer a bullet-shaped weight because it moves better over the bottom. Then I add two or three glass beads. Next I add another brass weight, usually a barrel-style weight. Now you want to tie the end of your line to the barrel swivel. This should be a fairly large swivel, about the size of the weights you're using. Next you want to take a piece of monofilament that's roughly three feet long, and tie one end of it to the open end of the barrel swivel. At the other end of the line you'll want to tie your hook. The hook I use depends entirely on what I'm throwing, but for the most part I'm going to use the same Trokar hook that I use in my double fluke rig (TK100 3/0) because I really like the low-profile design when using lizards and other large creature

Oneida Lake smallmouth.

baits, which is what I'm going to be using most of the time when I throw this rig. All these knots can be tied with a Palomar knot. The reason why you want the monofilament line for the leader is because you want the bait to try to stay up off the bottom just a little bit. Other than the lizards I already mentioned, some other favorites for me to use on this rig are flukes, tubes, ribbontail worms, and anything else that is long and has appendages that will move a lot underwater. That movement is great, but the biggest key to the success of this bait lies in the weights and the beads.

It is crucial that you use brass and glass because they make a clicking sound that attracts fish when they hit each other. No other combination of materials (plastic, lead, tungsten) will work as well as these two. Some people use colored beads, and colored weights; if I use any colored items I prefer them to be greens or browns to look like the things you might expect to see on the bottom of the lake. It's equally important to have that long leader because that will help keep your bait suspended off the bottom. I've also tried using a spybait at the end of the leader, but I haven't found the right length of leader to get the bait to respond properly, and my results have been mixed.

What I am looking for when I'm throwing this bait are fish that are pinned to the bottom in rocky areas. If I'm fishing shoals, hopefully it's a little windy, and I'll go the top side of the shoal and let the wind push me across the transition areas and just drag it on the rocky bottom. Because of the added weight, this is a particularly great way to fish when it's really windy and you're having a hard time finding a bait that will get on the bottom and stay on the bottom. What you'll want to do in this instance is cast with the wind, in the direction of your drift, so that once you have drifted to where your bait is, it will be on the bottom and you'll be ready to start presenting it properly with a few short tugs, followed by pauses in between. There's no need to reel in the bait, you can keep it on the bottom until you hook up or complete

Chenango River smallmouth.

your drift (unless you suspect that you've got weeds on your hook). If you try to cast behind you, into the wind, you'll find that you won't be able to cast as far, and the bait will have a hard time reaching the bottom because you're moving away from it. If I'm fishing points, or if there's no wind, I'll make long casts, wait for the bait to hit the bottom, point my rod at the place where my bait has landed and then do short little tugs to pull the bait on the bottom until I've pulled the rod as far as I can in the opposite direction of my bait, then I'll reel in the slack while I move my rod back to the starting point and repeat. Most of the time when smallmouth hit this bait, they do so like it owes them money, with no regret or remorse.

Gear:

7'-11" heavy- or medium-heavy, extra-fast-action casting rod; 8.1:1 or higher reel; 12 lb KIMURA Jim Root Fishing Monofilament line as a 3-foot leader tied to 65 lb braid

Weather:

Spring: Not a great spring bait, but okay for pressured prespawn fish, depth 10–20 feet

Summer: Hot, humid, high winds, clear water, water temp 70°F and up, depth 7–15 feet

Early Fall: Sunny, calm or windy, depth 5–10 feet

Winter: Not ideal for winter

When targeting fish around docks or laydowns you should be prepared to work fast and make multiple casts. These fish are generally not cruising, and can be positioned in such a way that they need the bait to come to them from a very particular angle in order for them to eat it. If you approach a dock from the south side and do the world's most perfect skip under it and don't get a bite, that doesn't mean there isn't a big fish underneath it. You could make several perfect skips from that side and get nothing, but move ahead and make one imperfect skip from the north side and catch a giant. It's also taken for granted that smallmouth live under docks because people are too quick to stereotype them as only living in deep water, so don't underestimate this tactic when looking for them, especially on hot, sunny, summer days. That's really when this bait is the most effective!

When fishing weedlines you'll want to try to position the boat on the deep side, parallel to the drop off. Cast the bait beyond the drop off, so that it lands on it, and then drag it until you feel it fall off. This is a great way to target suspended fish that are set up to find quick, easy meals and then return to the cooler, safer haunts of the deep water. Don't throw your bait directly into the grass. Instead try to work around or in between visible, isolated patches, so that your worm can be seen. This bait is great at enticing those finicky fish that aren't locked into one particular kind of forage, and by presenting it this way you allow them to see it from a multitude of angles.

Gear:

7'-6" medium, fast-action casting rod; high-speed reel 7.1:1 or higher; 12 lb KIMURA Jim Root Fishing Fluorocarbon line; Trokar TK97W-2 hook

7'-9" medium, fast-action spinning rod; 2500 series reel; KIMURA Jim Root Fishing 26 lb braid; 12 lb KIMURA Jim Root Fishing Tournament Grade Fluorocarbon leader; Trokar TK97W-2 hook

Weather:

Spring: Sunny, clear water, water temp 60°F–68°F

Summer: Sunny, windy, clear water, water temp 78°F and up

Fall: Shallow, clear water, water temp 50°F–60°F

Winter: Not ideal

22

Live Minnows

The first smallmouth I ever caught was on a live minnow. My stepbrother Dennis said to me "Come on let's go to Whitney Point and fish the spillway." I was probably in my late teens or early twenties, and I was really into fishing for big toothy critters at that time, but I figured what the hell, I'll give it a try. Besides, fishing with Dennis was always a good time. So we jumped in the van and headed over from my hometown in Oxford, New York, made a quick stop at a bait and tackle shop that's not open anymore called The Sportsman's Den, grabbed about two dozen minnow, a couple bobbers, and headed out. We arrived at the spillway, which is a discharge from a man-made dam at the bottom of The Whitney Point Reservoir that feeds the Tioughnioga River. That two dozen minnows probably lasted us about a half hour. We ran back and bought four dozen. We went through those in about two hours. Went back again, only to find they only had two dozen left, which we burned through in about twenty minutes. And just like that, we had caught about seventy-five smallmouth in just over four hours, highlighted by a seagull that managed to catch one of my minnows in-flight, during the cast, that I reeled in to shore and had to set free (thanks to the two older guys who were there to help us release that bird, unharmed).

How incredible is it that your first time doing something can be so perfect and action packed?! The funny thing is that trip took place roughly twenty years ago. Not only was it one of the most incredible days of smallmouth fishing I ever had, but it was the first and last time I would ever use minnows for smallmouth without having a young person with me. The reason is that I've been so programmed by tournament rules, and the inability to use live bait, that I've strayed from it entirely. But make no mistake, there is probably no better method to target smallmouth bass than minnows. Most guides bring two things on every trip with clients: minnows and crayfish. They bring these baits because they're as close to a sure thing as you're ever gonna get when it comes to trying to be sure you can catch something.

When it comes to live minnows a lot of people think that because smallmouth aren't four feet long, you have to use small minnows. But when I was in Minnesota we used red

Live bait is a great way to start kids. It's almost a guarantee that you'll catch fish, and the kids will want to come back again and again.

shiners, or reds, and some of them were six or seven inches. The bigger the bait, the bigger the fish, and the more likely you are to attract the attention of feeding fish. So I recommend that you go big. Use 5-inch shiners and a 3/0 or 4/0 hook. You'll want to hook the bait through the body, just under the dorsal fin. This will kill the bait faster than if you just hook them in the upper lip, but they'll stay on better when you cast and they'll swim very erratically, which triggers more bites. I recommend the smallest bobber you can get away with, and you'll have to test that with trial and error. If the fish and weight are pulling your bobber under, you'll need to go up a size. But you don't want to go so big that you lose bites because they feel it during strikes. As a general rule you can probably get away with something the size of a golf ball. If you need to go a little bigger you can, but you'll never need one as big as your fist or a baseball. That's overkill.

You'll want to use a splitshot for weight. This is a weight that you squeeze with pliers to cinch down on the line. You use this kind of weight because you want the weight to be between the hook and your bobber. I tend to put it about a foot above my hook so that my minnow has a limited range of motion. You also need to be sure that you use just enough weight to keep the minnow down, but not so much that it can't frantically swim a little or that it starts to sink your bobber. That panicking is what will attract the fish. If you limit it too much you won't get bit, and if you give them too much freedom they'll evade the smallmouth too easily. Half an ounce is all you should need, and you should place it about 12 inches above the hook. That will give them enough room to move around a little bit, but keep them down in the water column where you want them, rather than scurrying around the surface. You don't have to have a lot of line between your hook and your bobber. For one, if you have too long a leader you won't be able to properly cast without snagging something behind you. But also, and I keep saying this a lot, smallmouth will always come up. You can be 20 feet above them and get them to come to you. A 4-foot leader is more than enough. You can use this near ledges, points, rock piles, but one of my favorite areas to target is a channel of moving water where you can cast and watch your bait move in current. The key is to have current that isn't moving too fast. If you cast to 10 o'clock, it should take at least thirty seconds for your bait to move to 2 o'clock (as it would seem when facing the water). If it's moving slower than that, that's okay too. You just don't want it moving much faster unless it's on the edge of slow-moving water.

23

Ned Rig

You know that annoying friend that always seems to get the girl or guy, but you can never figure out what exactly they see in your friend? That's the opinion that a lot of people have when it comes to the Ned Rig. It's not fun to throw, it's not real sexy, but if you're in a river, particularly in the spring/early summer or late fall, and nothing else seems like it's working, it's a pretty safe bet you can get them on a Ned. It's not hard to throw, and not expensive, but it'll catch fish, sometimes it'll catch really big fish.

A Ned Rig looks like a small jig head with a small swimbait or finesse bait (think of a 5-inch Senko that you cut in half) but with a special jig head that's really lightweight (1/16–1/8 oz.). You can use a casting rod, but I think you're better off with a shaky head type rod, something a little bit longer, like 7'4" to 7'9", medium-weight, fast-action. The reason being is that you're basically going to be fishing it like a tube that you're slowly swimming across the bottom. You'll want to feel the rocks, which is why it's so important to use a spin-ning rod with fluorocarbon. This really is one of the few baits that's not really conducive to lakes or ponds, although you will find that you'll get a lot of bites on the fall because the Ned Rig has a very subtle drop presentation that you deliver on slack line, looking for a jump in the line to alert you when they eat it. When you do feel that tick, it's crucial that you not use a traditional hookset like you would if you were bearing down on a fish that just ate a tube. Because the

Lake Ontario smallmouth.

hook is so small, you'll want to just sort of gently pull on the line and let the fish set the hook on themselves or you'll rip the bait out of their mouth without hooking them.

Once on the bottom you'll be in the type of conditions where the Ned Rigs are really meant to be fished, bouncing as you reel it in current with no slack in the line at all. This type of presentation is a lot easier to control, and the fish will pull so hard when they hit the rig that they will set the hook on themselves without you needing to do it (especially with a spinning rod), similar to the way they hit a fluke in current. Because it's such a lightweight lure and you're using lighter lines to fish it, this is poor choice to use in thick grass or around laydowns where you'll have to try to horse fish, which is simply not an option with this set up or hook.

Also, I know I said it was meant to be fished in current, and it was (in my opinion), but it has to be slow moving and shallow (less than 7 feet) or the bait simply won't get down because it'll be too light and you won't catch anything. It's similar to a wacky rig in terms of weight and rate of fall, so keep that in mind when you're scoping out possible areas for you to use this bait. The first time I was introduced to this was by Russ Scalf on the Susquehanna River, and he had just learned about it from a guide on the lower Susquehanna down by Harrisburg where they caught several fish over 5 pounds on it mixed in with about thirty other fish from 2–4 pounds. So it's definitely a bait worth throwing in current. But due to the small logistical nightmare of finding the sweet spot for current and depth, it's really not my first option of baits to throw when the water is deeper than 7 feet. Ideally I prefer to throw

Russ Scalf was responsible for first teaching the author how to throw the Ned Rig.
Russ Scalf

it in even less than that, where I can get away with a little bit more current because it's shallower. It'll also help if you throw the bait upstream and let it come back down to you, rather than trying to cast to the side or behind, where the current can take you too far too soon.

For the worms, I prefer just a 3-inch Senko over the Z-Man products. I cut off the very tip of the fat end, so that I have a slightly fatter end by removing the taper a bit. This makes the worm a little shorter, and a little fatter. You don't want to go too small because this bait already attracts a lot of little fish as it is, and you don't want to increase that number unless you're just looking to go out and catch as many as you can, regardless of the size. Then by all means, cut another inch off the smaller end of the Senko so you have a stubby little 2-inch worm bouncing down the stream. My favorite colors are green pumpkin with black flake, solid black, and baby bass.

If you want to throw a Shad Shape worm or little swimbait you can do that too. Keitech makes a great little swimbait that fits nicely on the Ned Rig. I tend to use natural colors like Ayu, baby bass, and perch, but sexy shad is also a great choice, as is threadfin if you have those in the body of water that you're fishing. Threadfin shad are a huge draw for smallmouth, as are blueback herring, but not all lakes have them so you'll want to be careful when you're choosing baits to be sure you match the hatch. If you're not sure, stop at a local bait shop that has minnows and ask to see what they have in the tank. You can also look on the wall and see what baits they're sold out of. That's usually a pretty good indicator of what you'll find in terms of shad bait. It's not necessary to use jig heads here with eyes painted on them. Think of a 3-inch shad, and tell me the last time you saw one with an eyeball the size of a dime. Never. The mushroom head jigs in all black are your best bet. It's more natural, easy to find, and most often they cost less money but work better.

24

Cranking

Getting smallmouth on crankbaits can be incredible. When I talk about crankbaits I'm referring to a hard bait with a lip that dives anywhere from an inch (often described as a "wakebait") to a deep-diving bait that will dive to twenty-five feet. Most crankbaits float, so if you stop reeling them they'll start to rise to the top. These are the types of baits that I use. When I first started bass fishing seriously I liked crankbaits so much that my friends all called me JVD. I still keep one on the deck of the boat at all times because I have such ADD sometimes that I can't just slowroll or finesse fish without getting a little "chuck and wind" action every forty-five minutes to keep me sane! The biggest things to know about crankbaits are depth, water temperature, time of year, what the current feeding habit is in that particular time and body of water, and most importantly you need to remember what I said earlier: they'll always come up, but they'll rarely go down. This is crucial when choosing what crankbait to throw. Understanding how to properly use my electronics allows me to save a lot of time searching for fish to unlock this pattern. I'll idle over spots that I know hold fish in lakes, or around bends and deep holes in rivers, looking for layers of fish we call "lasagna." We use this term to describe the yellow, orange, and red you see from large schools of fish on the screen. When we see that, we choose what depth crankbait to use so that it will run just slightly above where they're positioned.

Your setup should be one of two things: Either a 7'-6" to 7'-9" glass rod, or a 7' graphite rod. When I'm fishing deep, the glass rod is

Releasing a smallmouth. Please practice catch and release as much as possible.

the best way to go because the fish will load up on that rod much better, and you won't lose as many. However, when I'm fishing shallow, around wood, or ripping through grass it demands the added backbone of the graphite rod. You can get away with a glass rod sometimes, but particularly when you're ripping through grass you'll find that you'll come through clean much more often with graphite than you will with glass. When it comes to line I like to use 8–15 lb fluorocarbon. The fluoro sinks, and you'll want that when you're using crankbaits. It also has a lot less stretch than monofilament, nylon, or hybrid lines. Braid is really not an option. One thing I highly recommend you use is a speed swivel. This will attach to the end of your line and allow you to change baits very quickly if you need to grab one that dives to a different depth, or a different color pattern. Many times when I catch a couple of smallmouth they'll either puke food they've eaten recently in the water as I'm reeling them in, or into the livewell while I'm storing them. When they do this it's imperative that you try as best as you can to match your bait to what they're eating, and changing baits within eight seconds as opposed to two minutes will allow you to have a hundred more casts throughout the course of a day. I also want to stress how important it is to have a rubber net. Treble hooks will get caught up in nylon very easily and you'll spend a long time trying to get them undone. Not only does this cause additional unnecessary harm to the fish, it's another example of how you can lose valuable time. My rubber net is one of the best investments I have ever made.

The type of reel to use is dependent the environment, depth, and location, but generally speaking a 6.6:1 is a great all-purpose reel for cranking. There are some instances when fishing deeper crankbaits, that you might want to use a high-speed reel to get down faster, but

Duel deep diving crankbait is another killer smallmouth bait.

once it's down you have to remember to slow down to a speed that will allow the fish to eat it. Will burning the bait quickly deliver strikes? Absolutely, but generally speaking you want the bait to move at a medium pace. Another reason why a 6.6:1 is a great option is because it'll allow you to slow down if you need to, but you can also speed it up to show the fish multiple presentations of the same bait. As far as the type of crankbait to throw, they're normally broken down by depth: wakebaits and shallow runners, medium divers, deep divers, and lipless. I started using the new Yo-Zuri Flat Crank in the spring of 2016 for smallmouth between 2 and 12 feet. Flat Cranks are crankbaits that have flat sides, as opposed to baits that have the more traditional rounded bodies. The benefit to the flat crank is that it has a much tighter wobble that is also more aggressive. You can feel the difference when you are retrieving the bait, and it generates a lot of strikes from fish that are actively feeding on bait by replicating a fish that is trying to run away, frantically.

For deeper baits I like the Yo-Zuri Deep Crank that will dive 12–15 feet. I like this bait a lot because it will actually get down to 15 feet, while most baits that advertise that depth don't actually reach it or, if they do, are only in that depth for a minute because you've reeled it in so far that it starts ascending back to the top. The Yo-Zuri deep crank gets down fast and stays down until it reaches the boat, and this is going to be key when it comes to targeting fish that are in that 15–25 feet. Fish that are deeper than that really won't engage with a crankbait. And to be honest, rarely will you get one in 25 feet to come up to 15 feet, but you might, especially if there's a suspended ball of baitfish above the lasagna. The last crankbait I throw is a lipless crankbait that's commonly referred to as a trap. My favorite is the 3DB Vibe S by Yo-Zuri because it has action that no other lipless bait has and the hooks are incredibly sharp. The best part about this bait is that I can use it in any depth. I can burn it across the top, let is sink and reel it slowly at a desired depth, or drop it off the side of the boat and vertical jig it. In any of these baits, my favorite colors are the prism series because they look incredibly lifelike and reflect a lot of light, which is exactly what a normal baitfish would do; my go-to colors are prism ayu, prism gold black, and prism crawfish. Those three baits in those three colors are flat-out devastating on smallmouth in any body of water.

As far as weather goes, I really have caught smallies on crankbaits in all types of weather conditions, all year, in varying depths of water, so I can't say that there's a magic window when you should be using a crankbait heavily. Right after the spawn, or deep in the summer are great times to throw deep-diving baits, and spring and fall can be great times to use square bills. What it really boils down to for me is the amount of fishing pressure the fish have seen from other anglers, and how aggressively the fish are feeding. It really doesn't have much to do with how much wind or waves there are, how much cloud cover, or how warm the water is. When you'll use each one of these will depend more on forage and stage.

WAKEBAITS AND SHALLOW RUNNERS

What does that mean? Well let's start from the top (literally) with wakebaits. Wakebaits, as I mentioned, run anywhere from 2–6 inches below the surface and tend to leave a wake behind them (hence the name). This can be a dynamite lure to use shallow for fish that are cruising the shoreline around sunrise and sunset, but it's even more effective to use on fish that are chasing baitfish to the surface. Earlier I mentioned this phenomenon in Chapter 7 on bird watching, when discussing how smallmouth will chase schools of bait to the surface. When this happens, the wakebait is one of my favorite baits because you can fish it quick, and it generates a lot of strikes from those heavily feeding smallmouth. My first smallmouth trip was at Oneida, and we had smallmouth-smashing baitfish at the surface all around us and none of us could catch them. I sat down disgusted after thirty minutes of failure, looked in my box and saw a wakebait. I tied it on, and the rest is history. Instantly my worst day became one of my best days. I can't tell you how many times I get messages from people sharing a similar story about how they saw smallmouth smashing the surface but weren't able to catch them and I ask them all the same thing: Did you try a wakebait? They all say no, and I tell them all the same story I just wrote, and the next time they have that happen I usually end up with about fifteen picture messages from them. The cool thing about this bait is you can use it to catch fish in as little as 1 foot of water, but you can also use it on those school-crushing fish out in water that's much deeper. That mental block of using a surface-area bait in deep water is tough for some people to overcome, especially if they've spent most (if not all) their life fishing banks, docks, and shallow grass. Simply eliminate the depth from your mind, fish like you would in 5 feet of water, and you'll have a lot of success.

Yo-Zuri Squarelip runs 3–5 feet and is a perfect prespawn or fall bait.

Shallow-running baits generally run from 2–6 feet below the surface, and are often referred to as "square bills." These can be dynamite baits to throw in the fall near creek mouths, or farther up in the creeks as the fall season progresses towards winter. Square bills produce a really tight wobble, and come in two varieties: one with rattles and one without, which is referred to as a "silent" version. The silent is really great for fish that are heavily pressured, but generally the rattling bait is the one that you'll want to use for smallmouth. This is a great bait to work around laydowns, stumps, shallow grass flats, river bends and banks, as well as when targeting fish that are on the bottom in 6–8 feet of water. I typically will use this bait when the wind is blowing real hard, or when there's no wind at all. These baits are really effective all year for smallmouth, and I caught the first smallmouth of my life on a sexy shad square bill.

You really can fish this bait in a lot of different ways, but ideally you want to slow-roll it. You don't need to burn it or worry too much about the depth. The smallmouth that you're targeting with this bait are feeding heavily, so you'll know right away if they're going to eat it or not because you won't have to show it to them too many times like you might if you were flipping or using a drop shot. This is really the best reaction bait ever made, and it will deliver some great numbers of fish year round, but the time to use it for big fish is in the fall when the fish are chasing shad into the shallows. This time of year you'll want to be sure to have all the usual color patterns like Sexy Shad, Tennessee Shad, and Grey Ghost, but the best color is easily Texas Craw. Rat-L-Trap came out with a flat-sided square bill recently called an Echo, and the action on that bait is pretty good when targeting smallmouth around wood or shallow rocks, but I like the Strike King or the Yo-Zuri for deeper water because they aren't quite as loud as the Rat-L-Trap and I think they get bit more often when targeting pressured fish.

Gear:

7' medium-heavy, medium-action casting rod (glass rods are best); reel in 6.6:1; 12 lb KIMURA Jim Root Fishing Fluorocarbon line

Weather:

Spring: Sunny, clear/stained water, water temp 50°F–60°F (pre- and post spawn)

Summer: Partly sunny, windy, clear water, water temp 70°F and up, any water depth

Fall: Shallow, particularly effective in and around creeks and creek mouths, any temp

Winter: Not ideal for winter

MEDIUM DIVERS

A medium-diving crankbait is one that will dive anywhere from 6–12 feet. This is a great way to target smallmouth all year long, and probably the type that I use most often. As a general rule I prefer the baits that will dive down to the deeper end of that range, say 8–12

Beautiful smallmouth bass caught on a Yo-Zuri flat crank.

feet, because I can employ a lot of versatility with how I work that bait, to allow me to target specific depths. For instance, if I'm fishing in 20 feet of water, I can bury the tip of the rod beneath the surface of the water to be sure that I'm getting that bait down as far as possible through the duration of the retrieve. But if I'm working a point, or over a hump, I can point that tip up to the sky and reel very slowly to keep that bait up closer to the surface.

Another reason why these medium divers are my favorite is because most of the time during the warm months I'm targeting suspended fish, fish that are near ledges, or that are chasing balls of bait, and this particular bait allows me to do that most effectively. The same is true for rivers, as the majority of them are not real deep (particularly during the summer), so it's really not very often that you can find a hole deep enough to run a crankbait that dives more than 12 feet. It's also not an overwhelmingly big bait like most of the deep-diving crankbaits are, so they're easier for smallmouth to eat, and to stay hooked on. When you're working this bait in a river, you'll want to cast upstream, and bring it down along a current break, or at an angle off the bank. The reason for this is because smallmouth will position themselves so that they're facing upstream, and while you can get bit sometimes by bringing the bait into the current, you'll be much more successful if you present it the way the fish would see it naturally. Also while I have just said that the best way to throw the bait is to bring it downstream, you should fan cast everywhere because the fish can position themselves so that they'll only eat the bait when it approaches them from a particular direction. This is very true for river fish, or fish that are in depths of 8–12 feet, and less true for deep fish.

Gear:

7'-6" medium-heavy, medium-action casting rod; reel in 6.3:1 or 6.6:1; 12 lb KIMURA Jim Root Fishing Fluorocarbon line

Weather:

Spring: Good for prespawn fish in and around ledges, water temp 45°F–60°F

Summer: Not ideal for summer

Fall: Great in early fall when fish are just moving in shallow, water in the 60s

Winter: Great winter bait in rivers

DEEP-DIVING CRANKS

Throwing deep-diving crankbaits for smallmouth can be some of the most fun you'll ever have. There's a lot of weight being applied to the rod due to the pressure that's being exerted by the bait as it dives, and the fish that are deep normally hit incredibly hard. So your rod is already bent, and pulling; compound that with a fish hitting your bait like a truck, and you get some really intense fighting. As I mentioned before, I highly recommend using a glass rod when you're fishing deep because that extra give will make sure that you get the best possible hookset with that fish. Essentially the fish will set the hook themselves.

What I do in deep-water situations is cover as much area as I can. I'll put the trolling motor up on high and start fan casting my way across an area, and then I'll work back across it again, then I'll move over and work across another area, and then make my way back again so that I'm zig-zagging my way over the area (normally it's a large group of shoals). This is a great technique to use at Oneida Lake in New York when fishing Shackleton Shoals. You can cover a lot of water and normally when you catch one

The author's favorite Yo-Zuri deep-diving crankbait. The prism maximizes light to create the best attractant.

there will be more there. Deep fish are generally schooled up very well and in common sizes. So the good news is if you catch a big one, there are probably lots of big ones there. On the other hand, if you catch a 2-pounder, that's probably all you're going to find in that school.

Once you hook a fish deep, your rod control is going to be the difference between landing that fish and losing it. You want to keep enough bend in the rod to keep the fish hooked, but you also don't want to lift up so high on the rod that you allow that fish to run toward the surface and jump. Try to keep the rod tip down, with the bend of the blank at roughly a 45-degree angle so that you're able to keep the right kind of pressure on the fish.

Gear:

7'-6"–8' foot medium-heavy, medium-action casting rod (glass); 7.1:1 reel; 12 lb KIMURA Jim Root Fishing Fluorocarbon line

Weather:

Spring: Not ideal for spring

Summer: Sunny, windy or calm, clear water use natural colors, stained water use chartreuse or white, water temp 70°F and up, depth 15–20 feet

Fall: Not ideal

Winter: Deep, slow-moving water, warm sunny days

LIPLESS CRANKBAITS

Lipless crankbaits are the most versatile of the group. You can use them to target fish at any depth because they don't have a bill, and they sink naturally at the rate of approximately one foot per second. Like the square bills they also come in silent versions, but I never use those to target smallmouth. Lipless crankbaits are awesome in any depth, under any weather condition, and at any speed. You can burn them across the top, slow roll them at a desired depth, or vertical jig them over fish you've marked in deeper water, and everything in between. In fact one of my favorite methods of using this bait to target big smallmouth is to rip it, then let it fall and reel in slack, then rip it, let it fall and reel in slack, and repeat this all the way to the boat. This is also one of my favorite methods and baits for targeting big smallies at Smith Mountain Lake in West Virginia near secondary points in creeks.

This bait is really best used for smallmouth that are feeding on large schools of baitfish, particularly when you see them busting at the surface. Because it's meant to mimic a bait that's frantically trying to escape, you really can't present it in an erratic enough way. This bait is really most effective for the three or four weeks directly following the spawn, and then again in the fall, but is also a great method to target those fish that are busting shad on the surface so it should be on the deck at all times during the summer. I've had numerous people catch their first smallmouth with me, but one of the most memorable was a good friend Ryan M, who was working for Stormr at the time and came for a visit to Upstate New York. We got into a school of smallmouth that were situated right on a current break that he could barely reach with his lipless crank, and that I could not reach with mine. The result was that he caught about twenty-five and I caught about two. I still hear about that to this day, and he refuses to go smallmouth fishing with me again so that he can keep that number intact. I simply did not have the proper rod and reel combo to get the maximum casting distance out of my lipless crank, and while

Yo-Zuri Hardcore Vibe is really great for deep water because it's heavy and you can cast it a mile, but it'll get down in a hurry when the fish are suspended deep!

I laugh at this story when he reminds me because it's funny, it's also a very clear reminder to me how crucial it is to have the right gear for the job every time you are on the water. Something that seems so insignificant at the time, will haunt you for years.

Before I close out this section I want to share a really great memory. When I had first started in the fishing industry I was doing some writing for *Fishhound*. They'd send me boxes and boxes of different baits to try and if I liked them I'd write a review. After I'd done a couple I got a box that only had one bait in it, with a note that said "One of three in the entire world. Don't post pics, and whatever you do, do NOT let the people at Tackle Warehouse find out you have this bait!" That bait was the Yo-Zuri 3DB lipless crankbait in Tennessee Shad. I took it down the Susquehanna river with my buddy Anthony and caught a beautiful smallmouth on it after only making ten casts. I caught one more after that, and then I lost it on a giant fish. I didn't have enough pics for the story, and I was really freaking out.

A couple weeks later I was at ICAST in Orlando, Florida, and went to the Yo-Zuri booth where I met Ray, someone who has since become a dear friend. I found the bait on the wall (this one happened to be just a demo, not a real bait), and I showed it to him and told him my story. His eyes were looking around the room and he kind of shrugged it off and said,

"There's no way you have that bait. You must be talking about something else." So I took out my phone and showed him my picture, and his jaw slowly fell to the floor. He could barely say "How . . . did . . . you . . . get . . . that? Can you please send that picture to me?" I did send it to him. And even though I'd been using their baits since I was a teenager, that moment started our official partnership together. Believe it or not, my life as a fisherman is full of moments like these, where things happen that have led to other relationships years later. That was 2014, and only now are those lipless baits just beginning to get the recognition they deserve. They're so good that many people won't talk about them. And the prism colors really are the best way to go.

Gear:

7'-6" medium-weight, medium-action casting rod; reel 6.6:1 or higher; 12 lb KIMURA Jim Root Fishing Fluorocarbon line

Weather:

Spring: Cloudy, clear/stained water, water temp 45°F–55°F
Summer: Partly sunny, windy, clear water, water temp 70°F and up, depth 8–15 feet
Fall: Creeks, clear water, any temp
Winter: Great bait to slow roll deep or to burn across points

THE CRANKING CONCLUSION

How you reel in each of these baits is totally subjective from one day to the next. Use different speeds until you find out what they want. Burn it once, then slow-roll it, then use a medium retrieve. You can try pauses when cranking, or slight twitches of the rod and speeding it up for brief moments while reeling. Sometimes these subtle changes in the cadence will be the thing that triggers the strikes. If you're marking fish but they're not eating, try a different color. Sometimes a green and white bait won't get bit at all, but a green and white bait with just a touch of orange on the belly will get smashed. You may also find that once you catch one, the others will get fired up and then you catch a lot.

25

Topwater

Sunrise and sunset are great for topwater, but are not the only times you want to throw it. Shane Durrance

Have you ever seen Shark Week, or any documentary on sharks when they're attacking those fake seals that scientists and filmmakers drag behind boats? That's exactly what it's like to fish for smallmouth with topwater baits, some of the most violently exciting action you will ever witness in freshwater. My son's first smallmouth came on a Yo-Zuri 3DB Pencil, and now fishing for smallmouth with that walking bait is one of his favorite things to do in the whole world. To be successful you'll need to have the proper gear, a few tips on presentation, and most importantly a little bit of knowledge regarding how they react to the bait, because it's not like any other style of smallmouth fishing that you'll ever do. Until this book I have avoided writing about this technique. So out of everything in this book I would have to say that this chapter contains more hallowed secrets than any other. I'd be lying if I said I didn't feel a little regret even as I am sitting here writing it.

Why so secretive? Two reasons: the first is because it's an absolute killer bait for smallmouth that most people either don't even consider or know how to execute properly; and the second is because there's no technique in the world that's more fun than this one. Why? Well remember when I asked if you'd ever seen an episode of Shark Week? Well, smallmouth react to this bait very similar to the way that a great white shark reacts to a seal. In fact most of the time you're going to miss the fish because they're not actually trying to eat it, they're ramming it with their mouth closed. They do this to stun the bait (hurt it), and they'll hit it so hard that the bait will actually lift up out of the water, sometimes as much as three feet or more. It's really quite a sight to see your bait fly up and to the left, and the smallmouth up and to the right. You'll even have multiple fish trying to hit the same bait. If you ever see me on the water, I promise you that this is the only time that you'll ever see me double over in laughter when I miss a fish. When they do miss it, 99 percent of the time they'll come back and try to eat it the second time because it wasn't an actual miss, it was an intentional strike to devastate that bait. For every fifty smallmouth that you catch on the top, you'll miss a hundred. So it's impossible to have a bad day when you're having this much action on the surface.

For gear you'll want a good long, stiff rod with a fast-action tip. Frog rods and flipping sticks tend to be really great for walking baits. The longer the rod the better because you'll be able to make longer casts in open water, and you'll be able to horse fish out of grasses and the other hazards fish love to run to when they're hooked. You'll want a high-speed casting reel, something that's at least 7.3:1 or better (mine is over 8) so you can properly keep the line moving on the reel during the retrieve. On that reel you have two choices: you can use braid or mono, or a combination of the two. In dirty water, I prefer to tie the lure to braid because braid floats very well, it's virtually impossible to break, and you can cast it a mile. In clearer water I'll use a monofilament leader of about four feet, tied with a double uni-knot. There are some people who spool the reel entirely with monofilament, but you really shouldn't do this because the monofilament won't last as long as braid, and if you get a good bird's nest in the reel you can pretty much cut all that line off. Braid will last all season, and if you don't use a leader you can use that same rod for frogs, jigs, punching, flipping, Carolina rigs and countless more. I'm a huge fan of having versatility in my gear because no matter how prepared you are, having another backup is always a good thing.

When it comes to the bait I strongly recommend that Yo-Zuri 3DB pencil. I have loved "walking the dog" for a long time. I started with a Zerra Puppy, moved up to a Zerra Spook, then fell in love with the Lucky Craft Sammy for about seven years until I got my first

Pencil. The first time out I caught seventy-five fish. So, to prove that it was the real deal I gave it to my buddy Matty to use on day two and I used a Sammy. He kicked my butt all over the lake and took the bait with him. The hooks are incredibly sharp, but what's most impressive about this bait is the way that the smallmouth respond to it. It was not designed specifically for smallmouth bass, but one day on the water with it and you'll swear that it was. For some reason the fish just can't resist it and once they're hooked they don't come off.

Using this bait is really simple once you get the hang of it, and you'll use the same style presentation in any body of water you're fishing. Make a long cast, reel in the slack, and then start working the rod in one of three ways. The first way has you snapping the tip down and to either your left or right side (depending on which feels more comfortable to you) at a rate of about twelve snaps every five seconds. You'll want to reel slowly as you do this, and you'll quickly notice that when properly executed the bait will zig-zag back

This fish was caught during the middle of the day in about a foot of chop on the water.

and forth across the top, darting from one side to the next. Now before I tell you the second way to present the bait, I want to say that I really encourage you to do it the way that I just explained because the rod angle will have you in the proper position to set the hook in the type of downward motion that you want to try to reduce the risk of losing the fish. You'll also be in a better place to fight the fish, with the rod tip pointed down (the tip of the rod might even be under water and if so that's fine, sometimes I will bury the rod as deep as I can to keep the fish from jumping). But because I've seen guys have good days with this other style I'll tell you and let you decide for yourself.

The second way to present the bait is to hold the rod vertically, and make snaps back towards you at the same cadence and rhythm. The guys I've seen do well with this claim that the action of the bait is better because the front of the bait is being pulled up instead of down. Have I seen it catch fish? Yes. But I have caught thousands over the years pulling it down, and I will not switch. I know that pulling down is the best way to present this bait. You have more leverage on the fish, less slack to try to recover when you do get a strike, and

This is another bait that you should try to cast in a sidearm motion to reduce backlashing. Russ Scalf

much more control of the bait if you want to speed it up. It's also much easier to restart when you pause (and you will pause) during the retrieve.

The last method, which sounds really unorthodox, is to just reel the bait in without any jerking of the bait at all. I discovered this by accident once at Oneida Lake when I thought that I had grass on the hooks and was reeling it in to get the grass off and caught a giant. When you have moments like this that seem like an isolated occurrence, you should absolutely throw that bait back out there and do the same exact thing again—which is what I did—and over the course of the next thirty minutes I caught twelve fish that way. I rarely do this, but there are times when this will get strikes that the other presentation won't generate.

Gear:

7'-9" heavy, fast-action casting rod; reel 7.1:1 or higher; 12 lb KIMURA Jim Root Fishing Monofilament line or 65 lb braid

Weather:

Spring: Cloudy, clear/stained water, water temp 50°F–55°F

Summer: Cloudy, slight wind 5 mph or less, water temp 70°F and up, any water depth

Fall: Cloudy, slight wind or calm, shallow water, any temp

Winter: Partly sunny, calm, water temp 40°F–50°F

26

Jigging Spoons

I remember being told that there was certain time of year when you had to throw a jigging spoon for smallmouth because it would get those big fish to fire better than anything else. I also remember trying over and over and never having one of those days and just being convinced that learning it was going to be the death of me. I tried in rivers, lakes—I tried every spoon you could think of. I even contemplated using the spoon in my silverware drawer. Okay, maybe not *that* level of desperation, but it was almost to that point. The thing is, I was doing it all right, except one tiny thing, and that tiny thing was the difference between two years of zeroes, and one day of nearly fifty fish and a 27-pound bag. Isn't it funny how that works, and how that "27-pound bag" got your attention like the first time you heard your son or daughter drop an F bomb?

So what is a jigging spoon? Well, it slightly resembles an old-school Daredevil if you remember what that was. I remember when I first started fishing that it seemed like all my friends had a red Daredevil in their tackle box. Also, I said for years that if any emcee ever asked me what I caught my fish on during a weigh-in that I was going to say a red Daredevil, and I actually got my chance in 2014 in Syracuse (thank you Chris Bowes). A spoon is a long, thin piece of metal that's shaped like an elongated oval. Most have at least one bend in them, usually around the middle of the bait. They can be as small as just a couple inches but traditional smallmouth spoons are about 4 inches long. Some have painted designs, but the plain silver spoon is the best bet for smallmouth fishing.

When I first went out with a spoon I had it all figured out. I had done all the research, all the prep, and I was gonna smash them, or so I thought. I thought I needed a cranking rod, 12 lb fluorocarbon, 6.6:1 reel, and I was *set*. First of all, that rod was a horrible choice because it had way too much give. The line was too light, and the reel was too slow. Basically, I couldn't have been worse off unless I had been using my son's Star Wars pole we bought for $19.99 because it came with a free Luke Skywalker t-shirt he wanted. Before a trip to Erie in November with Larry Mazur, he told me to be sure I had a heavy jig rod that was long, had

Larry Mazur with a giant he caught on a spoon.

heavy fluoro, and a fast reel. So I took a 7'-4", medium-heavy rod, 15 lb fluorocarbon, and an 8.1:1 reel and headed out to Buffalo. This time I thought I had it all figured out for *sure*. And then I saw his first cast and about died from disbelief.

The biggest key was that I wasn't working the bait nearly hard enough. This is probably the only time in my life when targeting smallmouth that I literally couldn't jerk the bait hard enough for it to be considered "too hard." That was what I was missing. But I never would have imagined that I would be doing what he did. We were drifting over some waypoints in about 30 feet of water. As soon as we marked fish he opened the bail and let the spoon fall. When it reached the bottom he reeled up the slack, and jerked the rod as hard as he could from 6 to 12 and then let it fall back to the bottom again. When it did, he again jerked the bait as hard as he could from 6 to 12. He let it fall again, and once again he jerked the bait as hard as he could from 6 to about 9, because the rod was bent in half with a 6-pounder on the other end.

That was the first cast, and the first of two 6-pounders that we would catch on that trip.

I could not believe how violently he had worked that bait. When I say you can't rip it hard enough I mean it. Most people don't even set the hook this hard. The only way he could give it any more than he did was if he came off the ground a little. I wouldn't have ever thought to do that because no other bait allows you to use it like that, which is why I never caught a smallmouth before on a spoon.

The other factor that I learned, which really we both figured out as the day went on, was how key the sun was to our success. Whenever the sun came out, those fish would fire on the spoon. When it slipped away, so did the bite. Also it's worth mentioning that the fish that were holding the tightest to the bottom were the ones that ate the spoon the best. We still caught a few that were slightly above the bottom, but we had a lot of confidence when we saw fish pinned. Especially fish that were alone because we knew they were going to be the biggest. Larry hooked one that I watched him fight for at least three minutes, which is a long time on a freshwater fish. The fish came off after the third time he tried to bring it to the boat. We all saw it many times, and it was definitely over 7 pounds. He worked that fish perfectly and I thought there was nothing more he could've done to boat it. Larry had a different opinion.

He was really upset, and said it was his fault that he lost that fish but that it wouldn't happen again and began to dig something out of his storage locker. He pulled out a single treble hook, and slowly slipped it onto the O-ring at the top of the spoon near the knot on the line. He held it up and said that no fish would come off now. He said when they choke

The best four smallies on the spoon that day.

it obviously they end up with two hooks in their mouth. But then they just eat the back hook, they'll still hook themselves a second time with the other treble and that's the key to keeping them. Even for a fish as capable of getting free as a smallmouth is, two treble hooks are really hard to escape.

The water was just starting to get right for spoons. At 52°F it was still about 6°F too warm. Once the water hits the mid 40s it's doable to catch anywhere from eighty or more smallmouth a day out deep like this in 25–60 feet of water. When you're fishing that deep it really is imperative that you have a heavy rod and heavy line. You want to eliminate as much stretch in the line as possible, and you need enough stiffness in the rod to be able to rip that bait as hard as you need to for you to be able to present it properly. You'll also need a little wind to break up the surface and help you cover water, but you want to be sure that your bait is dropping on the fish and that you haven't drifted away from your target by the time your bait has reached the bottom. You want to target rocky areas that are grass-free, but you don't want to have too many rocks or you'll get hung up in them.

Because of how hard you rip the bait, and how hard the fish hit it, targeting smallmouth with a jigging spoon is without a doubt one of the most awesome experiences you can ever have on the water.

Gear:

7'-4" medium-heavy, extra-fast-action casting rod; reel 8.1:1 or higher; 15 lb KIMURA Jim Root Fishing Fluorocarbon line

Weather:

Spring: Not a great spring bait

Summer: No no no

Late Fall: Ideal when the water is in the 40s, light winds, need sunlight, depth 20–40 feet

Winter: Great winter choice, light winds, need sunlight, depth 20–40 feet

27

Blade Baits

What exactly is a blade bait? I've heard that question many, many times. A blade bait looks somewhat like a side profile of a fish, but it's the thickness of a penny or less. They come in a variety of custom shapes, sizes, and color patterns. At first glance this bait looked like something I would find in a dollar bin. But after I did a little research I learned a lot about this bait that made me fall in love with it before I even threw it. To begin with, blade baits were really introduced to the freshwater world by saltwater anglers. They're designed to mimic dying baitfish, and their vibrating action can be used in a variety of presentations that will allow you to catch quality smallmouth twelve months a year.

Blade baits were the biggest weakness in my smallmouth game for the longest time because they require more tinkering than any other bait I've used for smallmouth. Unlike a crankbait or a spinnerbait, you actually need to adjust a blade bait depending on the type of water that you're fishing. If you're the type of angler that only fishes in deep lakes or rivers, then it's not a big deal for you because you can adjust the bait one time and not have to worry about it. But if you're like me, and you're so obsessed with smallmouth that you chase them from the biggest lakes to the tiniest mud puddles and creeks, you really need several that are well-labeled and

Blade-bait fishing can be really fun, but it often comes during the coldest days. Be sure to bring the proper gear!

adjusted accordingly. The last thing you want to do is bend a blade bait multiple times because you'll weaken the lure and eventually it'll break.

And honestly you don't need to do much to a blade bait that you're going to be using in deep lakes. It's really only when you're fishing them in current that you need to adjust them, and you do that because the current will manipulate the bait too much. By bending it a little bit you can have better control over how you work the bait in current, where you're really going to be limited to just shallow presentations because the weight of the bait becomes a limitation. Without the added weight, you get with a jigging spoon, you'll have a hard time reaching the bottom in an area of current before the bait is swept away to a different area. This does not mean you shouldn't throw this bait in a river because you absolutely should, especially one that gets a lot of pressure, because the action from a blade bait is unique and natural. Unlike a crankbait that relies on rattles, blade baits generate their sound from fierce vibrations that trigger fish both near and far.

This bait should always be thrown on a spinning rod. Remember it's very light, so you'll want a long rod with light line. I recommend at least a 7'-6" medium-light spinning rod, with 6 lb fluorocarbon line. Before we get into the tough presentations, I want to go over some of the easy ways you can use this bait. The simplest way is to burn it in shallow water like you would a square bill crankbait. The second is to use it around docks with a short pumping action of the rod to hop the bait with short darts. But it's really quite rare to use the bait in any method other than deep presentations in winter or periods of extreme heat in the summer. And this is when using the bait can be really tricky. You really need to keep the line pretty taut, even when it's falling, because if you allow too much slack you'll get into problems. The bites you're going to get will probably seem very soft at first, and if there's too much slack you simply won't feel them. Also, if your line isn't tight, the hooks can get caught in it and prevent the bait from being presented properly.

While you can use this bait in a vertical presentation like you do a jigging spoon, I actually prefer to slow-roll it like you would a spybait or a spinnerbait because it's easier to get the right tension on the line during the retrieve, and it's a deadly bait when the fish are

You will probably need to fizz your fish during blade bait season.

suspended. Keep in mind, there are certainly days, particularly in the winter, when the fish won't want to eat a real big bait like a jigging spoon, but still need that type of presentation to trigger strikes because they're pretty stationary and have very small strike zones. In the summer it's completely different and you can use this bait everywhere the fish are deep and feeding on shad. It's great for bridges, humps, or fish that are busting shad on the surface.

Keep in mind, however, that it's really important to take things like this that I say and use them only as tools to learn for yourself and not as rigid guidelines. Because the first time I used these baits successfully was in a river, in deep water, doing what I said was not ideal for this bait: vertical jigging in current. I still stand by that claim, but there are always exceptions and there are a lot of unknowns in river currents and deep holes. There could have been numerous under-currents there that I couldn't see that were keeping that bait vertical to my kayak. For whatever reason, I was able to drop that bait onto those fish and it worked out in my favor. But for every one day I have like that, there are going to be forty others where the first time I try I'll get about 8 feet of line out and notice that my bait has drifted down-stream 5–6 feet. This is evidence of that fact that time on the water is key to your success with any bait, but particularly with blades because you have to know when the water is right, when the fish are right, and when the conditions are telling you that this is what you need to do.

Warm days in winter can spark a blade bait frenzy!

28

Spybaiting

Many people that I know who have targeted smallmouth bass offshore have said the same thing to me: I found them today, but they were suspended. The implied message there is that suspended fish can't be caught if they're deeper than fifteen feet because few crankbaits will get deep enough and the ones that will are often way too big. This is when anglers who know how to spybait get really excited. Because most people don't know how to do it, and it will absolutely crush those suspended fish. However, not only is spybaiting the hardest technique I've ever learned for smallmouth, I found that it's one of the most difficult to try to explain to someone who hasn't done it. From a distance a spybait looks just like a drop shot, but you couldn't fish it more differently, and if you don't do it exactly right, you're doing it very wrong. This complexity is precisely why it's so rarely used, despite the rapid popularity it received when it first hit the scene. Everyone wanted to do it when they heard about it, but when they couldn't figure it out they just moved on. It's not hard to understand; if you hear from all your friends that they tried it but had no luck doing it, you're going to assume that it's not a great technique and you either won't try it, or you won't do it properly and will fail.

So why exactly is it so hard? Well to start with I don't think most people have the proper equipment. You really should only use a spinning rod. Spybaiting is a technique that uses spinbaits, which are very lightweight lures with props at the front and back of the bait. Spybaits are designed to target suspended fish, therefore they require very long casts that are next to impossible to make with casting rods. You'll want at least a 7'-6" medium-light rod, and a spinning reel with the lowest gear ratio you can find. Ideally you want something in the lower 5s like a 5.3, but even a 5.8 will do. For line you should use 6 lb fluorocarbon. You can probably get away with 4 lb or 8 lb, but I would not recommend 8 lb and higher because you're really going to be impacting the presentation too much.

The hardest part about using this bait is mastering the presentation. When I asked Brandon Palaniuk to explain it he said, "You have to learn the rate of fall and the rate of stall, to make sure the bait is always in the strike zone." That's about the best one-sentence

Oneida Lake, spybait smallmouth.

explanation you'll ever get. You have to reel the spybait so slow that watching paint dry might be considered faster. The first piece of advice I got was: If you think you're reeling slow, then slow down. You also need a precise understanding of how the bait sinks—the rate of fall—and how it looks when you're retrieving it—rate of stall—and there are only two ways that I can think of for you to really be able to fully grasp that. The first is to have someone very successful at it share time on the water with you, showing you step-by-step how to do it during the best spybait conditions so you can fully experience the cast, the wait, the retrieve, the bite, and the fight. If you're able to just call a guy like Brandon Palaniuk or Casey Martin and jump on their boat for a day, then you're in. You'll be the James Bond of the smallmouth world in no time.

For those of you who can't get a one-on-one lesson from someone like that, you need to explore option two, and that's a big, deep swimming pool. In an Olympic-size pool you can make a fairly long cast and count your bait down to at least 10–12 feet. I highly recommend not counting numbers because you can really screw that up and count too fast when you're on the water if you're anxious or starting to panic because you haven't caught any fish. Instead try repeating the same phrase, or sing the same song to yourself. Now, throwing a lure with hooks on it in a pool is probably going to require a little finagling, as most people don't see that as an acceptable form of scientific experimentation. However, this will also allow you to see how the bait moves in the water and that will help you understand so much.

Testing in a deep pool is really key, because there is a pressure component that you can't get in an above-ground pool. If you've ever swum to the bottom of a 12-foot pool, you've felt that pressure on your head and ears. That area impacts the rate of fall in your bait. If you think I'm kidding use a stopwatch and monitor the rate of fall in a 4-foot above-ground pool, and monitor it again in a 12-foot pool. Your rate will be higher in the 4-foot pool. If you just let that bait fall to the bottom of a 12-foot

The author's first spybait smallmouth, Lake Erie.
Jon Fuchs

pool five times, you'll be able to have a solid rate of fall for that bait that you can then use to determine exactly how long you have to wait for your bait to reach your desired depth. So if the particular spybait that I'm using (and many of them are different) with 6 lb fluorocarbon will hit the bottom in a 12-foot deep pool in twenty-four seconds, then I know that bait falls at a rate of 0.5 feet per second. Then I know that the fish I'm targeting in 20 feet will see my bait in forty seconds as long as there is little-to-no current or any other factor impacting boat position (things like current and wind can and will impact your rate of fall).

Because you're targeting suspended fish, it is crucial to have great electronics as well as a thorough understanding of how to use them properly. If you can't mark a school of smallmouth that are suspended at 15 feet of water on a 30-foot hump, your odds of successfully catching them are basically zero. You need to know how far to count down and how they're positioned; these things require precision and concrete data to execute. Once you have mastered your electronics you should be able to see your bait on the front graph. This will really help you measure your rate of fall on any given day to be sure that your bait is falling like you expect it to.

This is why most people fail. They don't let the bait fall far enough, and they don't reel the bait slow enough. Once your lure has reached the depth that you've marked fish in, you have to be able to keep it there while you're reeling it in. It won't do you any good to take the time to let your lure fall to 18 feet if you've reeled it up to 9 by the time you reach your fish. And this bait is meant to be reeled, not jigged vertically. This is part of the reason why it's so important that you make really long casts. Even with an open bail, your bait isn't going to fall in a straight line from where it hit the water. It is inevitable that the bait will slowly begin to drift back in your direction. Many strikes on this bait are caused by a territorial response. I think that sometimes people tend to not see smallmouth as the predators that they are simply because they don't have teeth. That misconception is one of the most ill-fated mistakes you can make when smallmouth fishing. Suspended smallmouth are normally in a very defined group (only 3-pounders, only 4-pounders, etc.) that does not accept outsiders. A spybait moving through that group at a snail's pace without a care in the world will get bit out of pure anger if nothing else. They'll hit it like they hate you.

29

Hula Grub

The Hula Grub, or spider jig, is one of my favorite smallmouth baits to use in the summer. It was first shown to me by my buddy Carl Sickles back in 2010 at Oneida. The Hula Grub is a soft plastic bait made by several different companies (I prefer the one made by Yamamoto) that features a skirt on one end and two crawfish claw-like appendages on the other end. I throw this bait on The Closer Shakey Head Jig with the screwlock attached to the skirted end and the hook secured between the two appendages. By rigging it this way it's completely weedless and can be fished anywhere: on rocks, in grass, shallow, deep. It is incredibly ver-satile with multiple presentations. Because it's a small bait, I recommend you use a spinning rod or a medium-weight casting rod. Either should be between 7' and 7'-6" inches. I would use a 10 lb fluorocarbon line, and either a 2500 series spinning reel, or a casting reel between 6.6:1 and 7.3:1.

I like to use this bait when I'm fishing lakes where the fish are scattered and they're not tar-geting schools of baitfish. If the smallmouth are feeding on crayfish, it's ideal. It's particu-larly effective on hot days when there is little-to-no wind and the fish are acting finicky and hard to pin down because it's the perfect bal-ance between a finesse bait and powerfishing. I'll use a variety of presentations until the fish tell me how they want it. Sometimes I'll work fast and use it like a jig and pitch and flip it around isolated weeds in 8–12 feet. Sometimes I'll throw it out and just leave it. Most of the

Big thanks to Carl Sickles for showing the author the Hula Grub and how to use it.

time I'm dragging it with rapid shakes of the rod to create the look of something hopping along the bottom. The last option for presenting this bait is to basically dead stick it. Just throw it out and leave it.

I mentioned previously how Carl Sickles showed me how to use this bait. That day was pretty memorable for me because it was my first step in beginning to figure out how smallmouth behave. It was very hot, and there was little-to-no wind, and we happened to see some birds diving while we were driving from one spot to another. When we got there and started fishing we saw a fish break the surface about 80 yards away. We quickly packed up, flew over there, and started fishing again but were unsuccessful. Ten minutes later we saw another fish bust about 50 yards away, we packed up and moved, and again we didn't get bit. This went on for about forty minutes and then we realized that the fish were actually all spread out. We picked a spot roughly in the middle of all the running around we'd been doing and just slowed down. Pretty soon we started catching one about every ten to fifteen minutes. We needed to slow down and let them come to us. This is why I've never forgotten the first time I ever threw the Hula Grub.

With river fishing I use it the exact same way that I do a tube. I look for current, and I bounce it on the bottom. For this presentation I really do prefer a spinning rod, because I tend to be able to have a better sense of feel with the bottom (probably from all my years trout and walleye fishing). The problem with that is having to fight smallmouth in current with finesse gear. Those bigger fish will own you. Because of that, I hesitate to use this bait in small rivers. Bigger rivers like the St. Lawrence are okay because you're basically fighting the fish in open water. The issue with smaller rivers are the things you can't see like the trees and other underwater hazards that the fish will run to. Needing to land the fish once they're hooked is really important, so take every precaution when choosing baits.

Gear:

7' medium, spinning rod; 7' 6" medium-medium heavy extra-fast-action casting rod; 2500 series spinning reel or casting reel 7.0 and higher; 10 lb KIMURA Jim Root Fishing Fluorocarbon line

Weather:

Spring: Great for pre spawn or post spawn

Summer: Great when fish are shallow (6–10 feet)

Late Fall: Not a great choice

Winter: Great winter choice, light winds, need sunlight, depth 20–40 feet

30

Scents

Using scents to target smallmouth is something that I've been doing for about four years. Scent plays one of the biggest roles in targeting smallmouth bass. Sense of smell is incredibly important to the fish that live in deep water. The next time you're at the lake or river fishing I want you to look into the water and ask yourself, "How far can I see?" In water that we consider really clear, you're lucky to see 10 feet. Most of the time, smallmouth live in water

Goby Oil smallmouth bass from Oneida Lake.

much deeper than that, in water that's nowhere near that clean. Now imagine how dark it is 25, 40, 50, or 90 feet below the surface. Even in direct sunlight, it's dark down there. That means the fish are relying heavily on their sense of smell, and if you pick the wrong scent you'll chase them away. Lucky for you I've used oils, pastes, pens, and sprays and I've found the ones that I think are worth trying. So to keep this simple, I'm going to just give you one example of each.

The first scent is called Goby Oil. It looks like Vaseline, and smells like death. Goby Oil is the only goby scent that I've found that is actually made from real gobies. It's made in Upstate New York by two guys, Dean and Rich, who catch the gobies and use a unique process to extract the oil from them. Because gobies have such little oil, it takes a lot of them to produce the container you buy. What sets this scent apart from the others is how you apply it. Goby Oil is not intended to be slathered onto your plastics and used immediately. Rather, you're supposed to apply one teaspoon of Goby Oil to a bag of baits and leave it in the sun or under a light for thirty minutes. This will transform the paste to a clear liquid. Leave the baits soaking overnight so the scent permeates the plastic. I've also heard of guides on Lake Erie applying a small amount of this to their drop shots. I've not tried this myself, but I can see how it would be effective under the right circumstances. I'll go deeper into the goby issue later, but for now let's just say that if you fish a body of water that has gobies, you should definitely have this in the boat.

The second scent is called JJ's Magic. I've been using JJ's since 2010. I use the clear liquid (it comes in a few different options) but this one is the only one I use. Unlike Goby Oil, this is designed for you to unscrew the cap, dip your bait inside, close the bottle, and cast the lure. Be sure not to skip that second-to-last step; JJ's Magic has one of the most powerful odors I have ever experienced, and if you spill this on the carpet of your boat you will be smelling it for the next two thousand years. It's a very concentrated garlic oil, and a little goes a long way. I love using this on my drop shot baits when the fishing gets really tough, when the fish are heavily pressured, or when the water is extra dirty. It might not seem like a lot, but a little of this on a Senko can make a huge difference and can be what transforms a terrible day into a killer day.

Next up is your Stick It pen. Remember those orange markers that used to smell delicious when you were a kid? Well this marker comes in chartreuse, but I would highly advise you against pulling the cap and taking a giant whiff. The benefit to this is that you can alter your bait a little to match the hatch and try to better replicate the forage. For instance, sometimes the smallmouth get really dialed into a perch bite and you can add a little color to a swimbait to make it resemble the bait more closely. Or add some orange to the claws of a crayfish to look like the pieces that were just spit by a smallmouth. These pens store really easily, but tend to expire faster than the other baits. So be sure to keep plenty on hand and stored in a Ziploc bag to maintain freshness.

The fourth scent I carry is Mike's Lunker Lotion. This comes in a red tube that opens like your kids' Crayola paint, and pours out the same way. When you apply it to your baits, it really needs help getting worked in unless you're using something hollow, like a tube or a craw. But that's actually the advantage to this bait; you can apply a ton of it and have it just sit there and slowly dispense into the water. For bedding fish, this is tough to beat.

Last but not least is a scent called Fizards. I first saw Fizards in 2014 at ICAST in Orlando. They gave me a free sample and I've been using it, quietly, ever since. What I love about this scent is that you can mold it, like chewing gum, and apply it to the hook and it will get hard like concrete. But what's really awesome about it is how it works. When you put your bait in the water, it starts to let out bubbles like an antacid. Each one of those bubbles contains scent. So your bait will actually leave a trail for fish to find it no matter where they are in the water column.

Before I end I want to say that any scent is only meant to enhance your baits. Before using anything I always start plain Jane, with nothing added. It's better to start with nothing and then start playing with oils or sprays. Traditional baits are still the way to go. If scenting the bait always worked better, baits would be sold with those scents already applied. Keep that in mind.

31

Mendota Rigs

The Mendota Rig is a reverse-weight design for flipping and pitching soft plastics. The idea behind this bait is that you can lead with the weight, instead of having the weight above the hook. This accomplishes two things: It reduces the weight you need, and creates a more lifelike presentation for your baits. By using less weight you'll have a smaller-profile bait that more easily penetrates mats and grass beds. You'll also find that you're able to enter the water much quieter with a smaller splash, almost like an Olympic diver. The smaller weight will also reduce the amount of times that fish spit the bait, as opposed to the bulkier punch rigs. Many people think it's a knock off of the Okeechobee rig, and while it's similar, it's a much better design.

The reduced-weight stuff is cool, but what I really like is the way that the bait functions in the water, and this is what generates so many strikes from smallmouth that see this bait. If you've ever seen video footage of a crawfish being attacked by a bass, it's not as if they go willingly. Crawfish will rear up in an offensive position with their claws in the air, ready to strike if attacked. Because the weight is in the back, and the head of the craw is where the line meets the hook, you're easily able to replicate this response by simply having a tight line, and lifting it slightly in the air. I've demonstrated this many times in public casting tanks and during demonstrations at ICAST in Orlando, Florida. When people see this firsthand they're hooked, and bass are no different. Smallmouth seeing this behavior triggers a fight-or-flight response that results in fights 99 percent of the time.

Mendota Rig skirted craw. You can clearly see the hole in the weight that the hook passes through.

The Mendota Rig comes in three options: skirted craw, craw, and a tube. The skirted craw is just like a jig at first glance, only you tie the line at the opposite end that you would a jig. The craw option looks exactly same, but without a skirt on the end. Both of these are incredibly lifelike in how they move, and in how they look. The third option is my favorite for smallmouth because it's a hard body tube. Whereas traditional tubes are hollow inside, this tube is solid. Having a solid body means that it's denser, that it'll last longer, hold more scent, sink better, and have better action.

When I use this bait I'm typically targeting smallmouth that are in that 7–12 foot range. I could absolutely use it shallower or deeper, but I like to be able to work it around isolated weed beds or on rocky points where I can work the bait exactly how I want. That gets more difficult the deeper you go because there's too much line out and you lose sensitivity with a bait like this over long distances and the presentation with it is *everything*. When I first got this bait I was blanking a lot and my frustration level was going through the roof. But one day I figured it all out and ever since, when the conditions are right, I can absolutely knock their lights out with this. The key to this presentation is cadence, patience, and more patience. I work this bait incredibly slow, almost like I do a fluke, but with the bait positioned in that raised defensive stance. I want as many fish to see the bait in this way as possible because it

Ontario bass can get a lot of pressure by the end of summer, and the Mendota Rig can be a key bait for you when the bite gets tough!

will trigger a competitive response in them. How many times have you been reeling in a fish that you hooked on a crankbait or other lure and seen a fish trying to attack the bait that is in the mouth of the fish that you're reeling in? Smallmouth recognize this stance from crawfish, and will respond, especially if they think that they're ambushing the craw from the side or if they can see another fish nearby.

I know that I'm making this sound easy, right? It's not. I can't tell you how many people have bought this bait because they saw pictures of fish that I caught, or pictures of fish caught by other people who understand this rig. Those same people will send me an email expressing a lot of frustration because they can't get bit, or can't figure out how to catch the size of the fish with it that I have. The biggest mistake that most people make is fishing it too fast. The most important piece of advice I can give you is to slow down. If you think you're fishing it slow but you're not catching fish, slow down. When my buddy Matt finally figured it out he said he casted it out, and started a conversation. It's not like you're waiting for the next glimpse of Halley's Comet, but if you're making more than one cast a minute you're on fast forward.

Now the second part is probably the most crucial, and yet you'd think it was the most obvious. The fish have to be in the mood. I can't count how many guys I know who are too damn stubborn to get out of their own way and will insist on trying to make fish eat something that they clearly don't want. If you're smallmouth fishing and it's two hours without a bite, you're using the wrong bait. I don't care who you are, where you are, or how many trophies you've won. Those fish are eating other stuff, and your Jedi Mind Trick isn't working. There are endless opportunities to throw this bait, but the best times are during the full moon from May to the end of September, because the crawfish are shedding their shells and the smallmouth will be feeding on them like crazy in that 7–12 foot depth range where you can maximize the effectiveness of this bait.

Gear:

7'-4" medium, extra-fast-action casting rod; reel 7.1:1 or higher; 12 lb KIMURA Jim Root Fishing Fluorocarbon line (4-foot leader); 50 lb braid

Weather:

Spring: Clear water, water temp 38°F–45°F

Summer: Sunny, calm, clear water, water temp 70°F and up, water depth any (variable weight)

Fall: Clear water, ledges, points, any temp

Winter: Sunny, calm, deep water 15 feet and over

32

Alabama Rigs

Since being introduced nearly a decade ago, the umbrella rig has been one of the most-debated lures in all of fishing. Now banned from use on the B.A.S.S. Elite Series, The Bassmaster Opens, FLW, Costa Series, B.A.S.S. Nation, TBF, BFL, and more, the more-commonly-referred-to Alabama rig remains a heated topic of debate among anglers. People who are in favor of using the bait tend to come from the point of view that supports innovation and the use of anything that has a hook on it in the traditional sense. Those opposed to this bait claim that it is bad for the sport, harmful to the fish, and "too easy" to catch fish.

Without getting into the moral debate I will say that in no way is throwing an A-rig a sure bet. I've used it, if it were still legal to use in tournaments I would use it, and I can promise you that it is anything but easy. First of all it's incredibly heavy. I can't think of another lure that you can throw that will wear you out like this will. Even the smaller umbrella rigs aren't easy to throw all day and the bigger ones will have your arms feeling like they're going to fall off.

For those of you wondering what the heck this thing is, the Alabama rig/A-rig/umbrella rig consists of one main head with multiple wires that branch off, each holding a bait. Each branch may or may not have a blade on it, similar to a spinnerbait. Now I'm sure that there are a lot of crappy fishermen out there that are nodding and saying to themselves that this is nothing new, and they're right. Pan fishermen have been using smaller versions of these for years. What makes

At Mille Lacs you're only allowed one hook, so use a three-wire rig there to reduce the odds of having false strikes to baits with no hooks.

this different is the size of the rig and size of the baits that are being used. The smallest A-rig is a three-wire rig, the most common has five wires, and it's really unlimited as far as the number of wires that one could potentially put on the rig (I've seen as many as four five-wire sets, totaling twenty baits on one line). Swimbaits anywhere from 3–5 inches and up are used on the end of each wire, attached with a jig head that weighs as little as ¼ oz. or as much as ½ oz., and secured with heavy gauge swivels on the end of each wire. When fully rigged, it mimics a school of baitfish swimming in the water. I've seen guys with five-wire rigs hook five fish on one cast. I've never done that. The most I ever pulled at once was three smallmouth, but all of them were in the 4-pound range.

When I got my first A-rig I threw it all the time. I bought what everyone was saying, and believed that all I had to do was throw this thing and the fish would be all over me. I can tell you that I probably threw the A-rig for three days before I finally caught a fish on it, and it was at least a month before I felt like I had any confidence in it at all, and I probably had arms like Popeye. You need to know what rig to throw, when to throw it, when to use rigs with blades and when not to, which swimbaits to use and what size, how heavy a jig head to use, what line to throw it on, what rod and reel, and where to throw it. To start with, you really only have brief periods of time when this bait is effective, and the biggest one is during the fall. After the second cold night, this bait is really tough to beat. Depend-

Austin Felix at Mille Lacs.

ing on the temperature and what kind of fall we have, this bait can stay red hot straight through December and into January. Once the water temps drop below 40°F it gets real tough to catch them on it. That leaves a giant window of about 30°F when it is lights out. My mistake was that I got it in June, so I spent months using it until I finally got to really see what all the hype was about. There are times in the summer when smallmouth will be keying in on balls of shad, and when they do this bait can crush them.

The best type of weather is always the same: windy, cloudy, nasty. One of the best attributes of the A-rig is that when the wind is really blowing hard, this bait will catch a lot of fish. In my experience the harder it blows the better. Especially when you use a heavier rig, like a Yellow Hammer Rig, and you tip it with ½ oz. jig heads and 5-inch swimbaits. This will guarantee that the bait cuts through the wind and waves and is able to get down to where the fish can see it. That's really great because heavy winds tend to be a huge turn-on for smallmouth, but getting down to them can be struggle. Not to mention it basically looks like a giant spinnerbait, which is pretty much my favorite smallmouth bait of all time. That being said, I do prefer the Yellow Hammer Rig because it's made in the USA by tournament anglers, out of the highest-grade components. This level of quality is definitely noticeable in the price, but it's well worth the money. The problem with cheaper versions is that they're cheap, and the arms will break off easily. Trying to handle one giant smallmouth is hard enough, and every time you add another it gets more and more difficult and the risk of breakage increases.

There's really not much to the presentation of the bait. You want it to stay up closer to the top (most of the time) and you want to reel it slow. You'll need to have a slow reel, like a 5.3:1. This is the biggest reason why people who try this bait fail. They use a reel that's too fast, and the fish won't eat it. Perfect example of that was when my buddies Matty and Johnny went down the Susquehanna together. Matty was catching them almost at will, and Johnny struggled all day because his reel was a 7.3:1 and it was burning the rig way too fast. You can only slow down a retrieve so much, and any reel over 6.5 is moving too fast. When you're reeling in the rig if they're not aggressively eating it during a slow retrieve, try altering your cadence a little bit. Reel slowly for five or six turns, then fast for three. Then slow for five, and fast for two. This little adjustment can trigger bites from those fish that are just trailing the bait from behind.

Having the proper line and rod are the other two parts to being successful at this. The line should be either a durable fluorocarbon that is twenty pounds or higher, or braid that is at least thirty pounds. Either of these will provide the durability that you need in order to throw this rig repeatedly. But, the most important part of this whole deal is the rod. If you don't use the right rod, not only will you lose fish during the fight, you will feel torn up after a very short period of time. Using the proper rod will reduce the lumbering that you'll do and make it much easier for you to handle the bait for a full day. When looking for a rod you want something long (over 7'-6"), with a long handle, magnum or extra-heavy, that will load up like a crankbait rod. This last part rules out flipping sticks, though a lot of people will try to use them and they'll catch a couple fish on it. The best rods to use are the ones designed for A-rigs, or for giant swimbaits larger than 10 inches because, while the bulk of the work is done by casting, reeling in an A-rig is still heavier than anything else you'll throw. These rods are designed to throw heavy baits that move, and to load up properly when fish bite the baits.

Gear:

7'-11" mag heavy, fast-action casting rod; reel in 6.3:1; 20 lb KIMURA Jim Root Tournament Grade Fluorocarbon line

Weather:

Spring: Mostly cloudy, clear/stained water, water temp 40°F–48°F

Summer: Partly sunny, windy, clear water, water temp 70°F and up, depth 7–12 feet. Not ideal

Fall: Cloudy and windy, shallow and clear water, any temp

Winter: Two-week window first part of January that is incredible if temps are steady and wind is manageable

33

Gobies

————————

Welcome to one of the most highly-debated topics in the North. For those of you that don't know, the goby is an invasive fish that came here from Europe. Large ships would fill their hulls with water to keep them stable while at sea, and then drain that water once they came inland so they wouldn't be as deep. When they let the water out, they dumped these small creatures as well, creating an issue that is being fought over heavily in some parts of the US, particularly the Great Lakes. As of today there are very few lakes remaining in New York that don't have a population of gobies. Once they arrive, it's freakish how fast they can multiply and have an immediate impact, and that is the center of the debate.

The biggest goby I've ever seen was just under 6 inches, but most of them are probably in the 3- to 4-inch range. When people hear this they immediately ask why they're such an issue if they're so small. The reason is because they multiply faster than any other species of fish I've ever heard of. Gobies will spawn an average of six times per year, depending on the location (approximately every twenty days). Essentially once the water warms above a certain temperature they'll start spawning and will continue to spawn until the water drops back below that point (that temperature is relative to different bodies of water). As this spawning process unfolds throughout the course of the year, the males will change color from brown, to green, to black, and their odor will increase, similar to that of a rutting buck in the fall. This makes them a primary target for smallmouth, and one that is easily locatable for them. Once the four-year-old male finishes guarding the eggs, he will die (females will also only live to about three to four years of age). During reproduction, mature females will deposit anywhere from 90–3,900 eggs each time they spawn. Just think about that, and how explosive this can be in terms of growing numbers overnight, and it's easy to see why some anglers would have huge concerns for fear that these little critters will be eating all the smallmouth eggs (actually their preferred primary forage is zebra mussels, another invasive species to the Great Lakes and other bodies of water),

What wasn't expected though was the rate at which the smallmouth would eat and digest these tiny balls of deliciousness. As it turns out, gobies are incredibly high in protein, and because of their lack of bones smallmouth are able to digest them easily and rapidly. The question then becomes, can they eat them so readily that they can keep the fishery from becoming overrun with them? At this point it's unclear. What is obvious is that smallmouth that are feeding on gobies as at least a part of their diet are exploding in size, almost as fast as the goby population is. I'll give you two examples of this. The first is Oneida Lake. We all knew that Oneida would be infested at some point because it's connected through the lock system, so there really was no way to prevent gobies from coming in from Lake Ontario and the St. Lawrence River. The first time I saw one there was in 2014 while fun fishing with Brandon Palaniuk. We were out on the east end, in an area that was marked by a large sand bottom. Brandon mentioned that he had caught a couple in that area once before and couldn't understand why because there wasn't any rock or ledges that would typically hold big smallmouth in that area, but thought we should check it out anyway. On his second cast with a drop shot he reeled in something small. When he held it in his hand he started jumping up and down with excitement. He said that this lake would explode, that it set up perfect for big smallmouth, and that in five years it would be one of the best smallmouth bodies of water in the world.

Fast forward two years later to the first Northern Open of 2016 when a lake that has been dominated by winning bags of largemouth weighed in approximately 90 percent small-mouth bass, and all but one of the boats on the final day were anglers targeting smallmouth. The largemouth weren't a factor at all, and that has never been the case at Oneida prior to 2016. The smallmouth have always been easy to catch there, but 2-pounders weren't winning tournaments and the bigger ones were harder to find than the largemouth. Now, it seems like anyone can find a school of 3-pound smallmouth, so 15 pounds a day isn't the same guaranteed check that it used to be. In the fall of 2015 I caught the biggest five-fish limit of smallmouth of my life from Oneida, and I didn't share any pictures from that day for two reasons: 1) Nobody would have believed I caught fish that big there; and 2) I didn't want people to know that I caught fish that big there.

The other place where you can really see the impact that the goby has had is in the tiny Chenango River, in Upstate New York. This river runs less than 60 miles, and holds only one stretch that's less than 5 miles long that can be navigated by bass boat. For the most part it's incredibly shallow, and full of big pike, musky, and brown trout (at the north end). It's been a place where we could go catch fifty smallmouth a day, but they were normally small. No smallmouth have ever been stocked there by the state, and nothing is done to try to make it flourish as a smallmouth fishery, so what you see has been done by Mother Nature alone.

This spring I noticed that we were catching some of the biggest smallmouth I've ever seen in that river. Every time we went we were catching fish in the 3–4 pound range, which is an incredible river fish (remember, current smallmouth will never attain the same size as Great Lakes smallmouth, but are pure muscle). My buddy even commented on how shocked he was at the fish we were catching there and how it seemed like all the small ones just blew up overnight. Then two weeks ago I got a text from Ron's son Trent, and it was a picture of goby he caught in the Chenango and it all made sense. What's strange is that I couldn't imagine how those gobies found their way into the Chenango. But if they're in that little river, there's about a 99 percent chance that they're in every single body of water in New York. If not, they will be soon, and the smallmouth will indicate when they've arrived.

The arrival of gobies will change smallmouth migratory patterns a bit. Traditionally people always looked for smallmouth in areas of current, rocks, and gravel. These are all great places for gobies to spawn, but after that they prefer the sand, and the smallmouth are adapting and are hunting them in these areas. The Donkey Kong Rig section in the swimbait chapter gives you detailed information about how to find smallmouth that are feeding on gobies in the sand, and you have to understand how to do this if you're going to be the best you can at finding and catching the biggest smallmouth.

PART III

Smallmouth Locations and Anecdotes

34

My Top Twenty-Five Smallmouth Destinations

I've tried my best to fish the best smallmouth waters in the world. This list is based on criteria I created to generate a score based on number of fish I caught in a three-day window and the number of fish over 4 pounds. From what I've seen and where I've been, here are my top twenty-five.

#25 Lake Coeur d'Alene, Idaho

"I'll admit you're right about Mille Lacs having more 4–6 pound smallies than anywhere else, but *nowhere* will you find more 7- to 9-pound smallmouth than here in Idahome!"— Brandon Palaniuk, when he sent me a picture of the 7.45 giant he caught in the fall of 2016. Expect to see some pictures of him and me with huge smallmouth in the fall of 2017.

#24 Wisconsin River, Wisconsin

If you've tried to sink your fiberglass boat and failed, this is the place to go. All joking aside, the Wisconsin really is an incredible fishery, but like most smallmouth streams you really shouldn't access this with anything other than a jet boat, and probably not one much bigger than seventeen feet. I wasn't sure if I should be excited or terrified when we were running, but the smallmouth we caught were incredible and I'd do it all over again tomorrow. My favorite bait here is a small white-and-chartreuse spinnerbait with one gold Colorado blade.

#23 Delaware River, Pennsylvania

Ever since my brother moved to Pennsylvania we've had to take our summer fishing trips in the Poconos, and that means a lot of exploring the various sections of the Delaware River.

Delaware River rapids should be treated with caution.

While this is a honey hole for many trout lovers, the smallmouth here are big, mean, and absolutely thriving. However, most of this water is only accessible in a raft, kayak, or canoe, and should never be navigated when the water is below 60 degrees, limiting the access to just a few short months from late spring to early fall. During this time you'll want to focus on the deeper holes that have quick-moving outlying areas of current. If you want to try to fit in with the locals you can bring a fly rod and big, white streamer.

#22 Chenango River, New York

Without a doubt there are going to be at least twenty people who will consider hiring a hitman to take me out if they find out I put this river on this list. There's really only one stretch about 5 miles long that will allow you to launch and fish a fiberglass boat, but that stretch has yielded over fifteen 20-pound bags for me in the past three years. That's remarkable for a river this size that is never stocked with smallmouth, and that floods terribly at least once a year. Most of the water in that stretch is over 10 feet deep and littered with rocks. Firetiger crankbaits and brown with black flake tubes are the best baits here, with spring and fall being absolutely incredible.

#21 Pepacton Reservoir, New York

Most of the people that I know aren't willing to trade in their outboard and expensive electronics for a day to take a canoe or small johnboat to a place this big, but those who have done it do it again, and again, and again. In fact, if this place ever does open up to large boats and motors (it's a waterway for New York City with incredibly tight restrictions that limit access) you will see weights of fish that you didn't even think were possible for smallmouth in any lake, let alone in New York. When it's really hot in the summer and the water has fallen due to drought, you can actually see the tops of old churches and buildings still standing beneath the surface from towns that existed before they dammed this area. I'm not kidding when I say that I wouldn't be surprised if the world record smallmouth was caught here one day.

#20 Smith Mountain Lake, Virginia

This is another one of those lakes that makes you stop and admire how lucky you are to be alive. The scenery is amazing, and the winding rivers of the Blackwater and the Roanoke are full of big, beautiful smallmouth. This is not only home to two of my best friends (Tyler and Zach Meadows), but is also where I met Destin Demarion, with whom

Sunset on the Chenango River, where the author learned how to fish.

I've spent countless fishing hours. The dam here does pull current on a daily basis, and while it isn't really noticeable to you, it is to the fish, who will immediately run to the deep and pin to the bottom, making themselves ripe for the drop shot picking! Drop shot a Roboworm or twitch a Yo-Zuri Prism Ayu Jerkbait. Spring can be great too, and red clay banks hold lots of fat prespawners.

#19 Chautauqua Lake, New York

This place is nowhere near as good as it used to be, but it's still one of the best smallmouth bass fisheries in the world! Ten years ago if you fished a tournament here you wouldn't cash a check if you had a green fish. Now most bags are all green with just an occasional smallmouth, but there are still plenty of big ones here if you know where to look in the middle part of the lake. The fall is really the best time, but with Dunkirk (Lake Erie) just fifteen minutes away it gets overlooked a lot. Even I only fish here when the wind blows me off of Erie, but how awful is it to get blown off of one world class lake and onto another? Carolina rigs and tubes out in the deep areas and around the bridge can produce *giant* smallmouth.

#18 Lake Winnipesaukee, New Hampshire

With just under 260 islands, there is no shortage of structure at Winnie, and you can catch a pile of smallies here and 4-pounders aren't too hard to come by. Not to mention the scenery is one of the most incredible that you'll find anywhere, particularly in the fall. Springtime drop shot fishing is some of the best you'll find.

#17 Dale Hollow Reservoir, Tennessee/Kentucky

To be honest, I didn't do any research about this lake before I fished it, and I don't know if that's good or bad. Only after I left did I learn of the giant that came out of this place, but I can clearly see why: structure, current, tons of forage, and the perfect climate to grow giant smallmouth. If you live in the South and don't have the time to drive north but want a legitimate shot at a smallmouth over 6 pounds, this is your place. Red Texas Craw Square Bills around rocky points are highly effective.

#16 Rice Lake, Canada

My good friend John McGoey lives on this lake, or I wouldn't have heard of it myself, but boy am I thankful that I have. This place is 100 percent what you would expect from a Canadian smallmouth fishery: big, clear water and giant fish. The first week of July here is epic, and absolutely the place to bring your shaky head and your deep-diving crankbaits.

#15 Lake Champlain, New York/Vermont

The north end of Lake Champlain, most notably the part known as "The Inland Sea" near the New York/Vermont border is perhaps the most beautiful place I have ever seen. The water, the boulders, and the tree-covered islands are second only to the smallmouth that can be found there. While there are many parts of Champlain that will allow you to fish with either a New York or Vermont license, this section is Vermont-only, and is a great place to work a fluke.

Lake Champlain can have storms as big as the fish!

#14 Douglas Lake, Tennessee

If you know my history then you're probably a little surprised by this, being that it was the location of my first ever ZERO and it came on the biggest tournament of my life while being filmed by The Weather Channel during a B.A.S.S. Open in 2014. But what you might not know is that at that time the Tennessee game commission was still trying to grow the smallmouth population and had set up strict size limits. As a result of those limits I was unable to weigh in any of the 4-pound smallmouth I caught. Had I been able to weigh them I would have had over 20 lbs. Today the smallmouth are thriving, and when they lower the lake to summer pool it's a slug fest! But don't go when the water's up or without the Tennessee Valley Authority app. A-rigs are a must here.

#13 Kentucky Lake, Kentucky

I love this lake. It's not only beautiful, but the smallmouth are just psycho. If you've ever wanted to learn how to use a spoon, this is the place to do it. I would highly recommend this lake to anyone with a love for smallmouth fishing. You can find them anywhere, so it

The sunsets in New York can really be incredible. Oneida Lake is on the rise and will only get better over the next ten years.

will really allow you to fish your strength, but the bigger fish are deep for sure. The fish here will eat just about anything, but you'll hit the motherlode with a lipless crankbait when the birds are diving!

#12 Oneida Lake, New York

Since the infestation of gobies into Oneida, the smallmouth bass have exploded. Not only are there tremendous numbers, but the lake sets up perfectly to be one of the best smallmouth habitats in the world and with the rates that these fish are growing, you're going to be reading a lot about the smallmouth that are being caught here in the next five years. In one trip here last fall I had two fish over 6 pounds in one day. It's impossible to go here and not catch a smallmouth over 3 pounds, which for a lot of people is the biggest smallmouth of their life.

#11 Lake St. Claire, Michigan

This place is smallmouth factory! For years during tournaments here guys made the run to Erie. Now, coupled with some great conservation efforts and many of those fish from Erie having found new homes near the weigh in, St. Claire is quickly becoming one of the better smallmouth bodies of water in the world. No smallmouth bucket list is complete without a stop here, so bring your drop shot rod and look for offshore structure to bag your limit and have a chance at a true trophy. Be sure to bring your Slammers and Erie Darters.

#10 Susquehanna River, Pennsylvania

The Susky is a great body of water and not a place to take lightly. If there's any negative to the Sus it's that smallmouth over 5 pounds are extremely rare, but we're talking about river fish, not lake fish, and fighting a 4-pound smallmouth in the current of a river will ruin you. Some of the best places to fish are dangerously shallow and should only be approached with a jet boat, and even then you really should take a trip with a guide first to learn the area before trying it yourself. Longlevel and Goldsboro are both places that set up like lakes and have deeper water for fiberglass boats, but the biggest schools of fish that offer up a chance at a one-hundred fish day require a jet or years of knowledge to traverse. The Double fluke rig is almost unbeatable here.

#9 Keuka Lake, New York

This lake is by far one of the smallest smallmouth bodies of water, but the fish here are gorging themselves on trout and have the size to back it up. In a double-shot tournament in 2015, five teams weighed in over 22 pounds *twice*. That's an astounding ten 5-fish limits with each fish weighing an average of over 4 pounds. I have never seen another place on earth with that amount of fish. In the spring, there's no question that you can catch eighty fish a day working the shoreline with a swimbait. Ted's Tackle is a great place to get your baits and local knowledge, too.

#8 Candlewood, Connecticut

"The Wood" might not be the biggest body of water, but it is *loaded* with smallmouth bass. Not only that, but there are some giants there! It's also one of the best places to target smallmouth through the ice. If you're going to this lake make sure you have the Humminbird Lakemaster chip, and be prepared to flip a jig, a lot. This lake also has an early season that opens around April 1 so you can get your fix from a long winter before you can in a lot of other places. Be sure to bring your drop shot rod with a pink Senko.

#7 Pickwick Lake, Tennessee

Out of all the lakes in the South, this is the one place I've found where the smallmouth will fight like they do in the North. Combine that with some five-fish limits that have topped the 30-pound scale and you have one of the most incredible smallmouth fisheries in the world. A Tennessee Valley Authority lake, Pickwick is full of current, and if you're not able to understand it or have the unfortunate bad luck of arriving when they don't pull current during your stay, you will most likely miss out on the magic of this body of water. So for those reasons it's ranked seventh, but for pure size it is right up there against any other smallmouth body of water. Also happens to be my favorite place to throw topwater.

#6 St. Lawrence River, New York/Canada

I'm telling you right now that in my opinion, the best freshwater fishing you will ever see in your life is the third week of June in Clayton, New York on the St. Lawrence River. Not only can you easily catch over a hundred fish per day, but there is unlimited potential for 5- and 6-pound smallmouth. The best part is that you can catch them with reaction baits like swimbaits, drop shots, and spinnerbaits, and the fish are in a feeding frenzy. This week alone makes this a top-ten fishery, and the fall can be stellar as well. Never go here without a Strike King Sexy Shad Tour Grade Spinnerbait!

Also known as the Thousand Islands, the St. Lawrence River can be one of the best smallmouth experiences of your life.

#5 Lake Ontario (Eastern Basin), New York/ Canada

Chaumont Bay, Henderson Harbor, and Sodus make the eastern side of Lake Ontario one of the most compelling smallmouth bodies of water in the world. With numerous islands and bays to hide in, there's rarely a day where you can't fish

The Eastern Basin of Lake Ontario, Big Momma's House, is my home away from home.

safely from winds that can deliver some intense nautical conditions. Tubes are the best way to target fish here all year long, and your best bet at landing a fish over 6 pounds.

#4 Lake Simcoe, Canada

It wasn't an easy choice deciding on which lake would be number one. I caught the biggest five-fish bag of smallmouth in my life on Lake Simcoe, but the numbers of fish were hard to find. It's also not an easy place to access, being that it's the farthest north of all the lakes and requires a border crossing that can be a giant pain in the butt. It's also incredibly cold and can have some horrible wind so you'll want to take every precaution when visiting. If you want to catch a smallmouth over 7 pounds this lake offers one of the best opportunities to do it. Swimbaits for days!

#3 Northern Michigan

I have never seen a more beautiful assortment of lakes in my entire life. We fished seven lakes in three days, all of them within minutes of each other. Every one had smallmouth over 5 pounds, and a couple of them were so clear that it looked like the Caribbean. Lake Michigan

Easily one of the most amazing smallmouth experiences of the author's life was here. If you haven't been, you haven't lived.

Taking two big girls out of the livewell in Traverse City.

Lake Erie sunrise. John Fuchs

Matty and the author at Mille Lacs.

and Huron are the biggest, but Traverse City is quickly becoming world famous and now I see why people in the know are convinced that is where the next world record will come from. The recent state record was just set at 9.98 pounds. On a nightcrawler . . . *doh!*

#2 Lake Erie, Eastern Basin

Lake Erie is home to numerous state record smallmouth and has tremendous structure to help them survive. Like all of the Great Lakes, the wind and weather keep people off it most of the year which helps to make the fish there easy to catch. My favorite technique here is dragging a Donkey Kong in the sand.

#1 Mille Lacs

When I walked off the water after my third day here I shot a 15-second video that simply said "I don't care who you are, or where you're from, Mille Lacs is the greatest smallmouth fishery in the world." By the end of that short clip, I was smiling so big and laughing so hard that I could barely finish what I was trying to say. I'll go here every year for the rest of my life.

35

Lake Erie, Buffalo

Did I not say at least five times already that you need to check the wind and wave report before going out on Lake Erie? This is particularly true for the Eastern Basin, where in most cases there is no place to hide if the wind is bad. I've been there at least a dozen times, and could have written about any one of those magical trips for this book, but I wanted to give a detailed retelling of this lake, which meant a fresh trip. So, I spoke with Larry Mazur, and we finally found a day that looked to be okay in the morning—higher winds forecast in

A nasty wind storm brewing on Lake Erie.

the afternoon might make it too rough and force us in early, but at least we could get that early-morning bite. I called my buddy Anthony, and the team set its alarms for 1:00 AM. The following is my account of the events.

I don't even sleep. I'm so excited that I watch old episodes of *America's Got Talent* until 12:45. Get up, splash some water on my face, get dressed, throw my gear in the truck, grab Anthony and we're on our way west. It's a four-hour drive to meet Larry, and we need to be there by 5:30. I'm checking the weather obsessively the entire way there. Wind is 4 to 5 mph from the East (perfect, actually), and the wave report indicates typical 1–4 foot waves, with no small-craft advisory, so everything looks good. Even when we're less than five minutes from the launch, the leaves aren't moving at all on the trees, and the sky is just starting to turn orange and yellow. Then I get a text from Larry: "It's whippin', dude."

No way. I tell myself that he's messing with me. But when I get to the launch, it's blowing a consistent 30 mph. Out at the far end of the harbor I can see the waves crashing over the breakwall. They have to be at least 8 feet for that. Devastated. There's nothing you can do in this situation. We pack it up, make the four-hour drive back to Binghamton, and try again a week later.

A week later and with much calmer winds, it's on. Anthony isn't able to come with me, but I grab Matty this time and I know he's excited to fish Erie for the first time. Not only that, but we've had a crazy week that started with a day at Oneida on Wednesday, drove four hours to fish Candlewood on Thursday, then drove eight hours to Erie Thursday night. It's totally insane, but this is what I do to chase the biggest smallmouth there are. Anthony started calling us #TeamNoSleep. It stuck.

So Matty and I arrive at Dunkirk, again, this time the wind is still pretty bad, but we decide to go anyhow. This day will be the first time that I get seasick in over seven years. I don't puke, but I'm damn close and because of it I don't eat or drink anything all day because I know if I do, it'll come right back up. We head out to multiple spots. The waves are big, but they're wide rather than tall, so it's not nautical or anything. All together we fish over twelve different waypoints, and mark probably two thousand fish. We throw drop shots, spoons, tubes, and crankbaits. There are probably over ten thousand fish caught in our lifetime when you total them all up between Larry, me, and Matty. In a place we've fished over a hundred times, and won over $100,000 (Larry won an Everstart here in 2011). And despite all that, we zero.

That's hard to admit, and I could have left it out. But I want you to understand as a reader that it's not easy to fish here sometimes. There are days when the fish feed all at once, or only on very specific baits. That day just wasn't meant to be our day. But two months later we'd return to Erie, this time out of Buffalo, and it would be a very different day.

We launch out of the old NFTA, which is now called Small Boat Harbor. It's undergoing a lot of reconstruction at the time we are there, which makes navigating to the ramp a

Still windy, but not nearly as bad as the author's first two trips.

bit tricky, but we finally find a spot near Charlie's Restaurant. I remember this spot well. I fished a two day Eastern Regional Championship here once in October that was so bad that we weren't allowed to fish the lake on day one because the waves were crashing over the breakwall. Half the field zeroed on day one, including myself, having never spent one day in the Niagara River at that time (a mistake that I have since corrected and have found a lot of confidence in that river). Day two they allowed us to fish a portion of the lake, and I fought my way back into the top fifty by the skin of my teeth, which allowed me to qualify for the National Championship for the first time. So you could say this is a pretty special place for me. It's also where I learned to throw the Donkey Kong Rig with Larry.

It's pretty perfect that day. There's about one foot of chop on the water, and it's partly cloudy. Water is 52°F degrees, so it should be game time. Larry catches a 5.5-pound smallie on his first cast with a spoon, and I catch a 5-pounder on a drop shot about five minutes later. When the sun is out, the fish fire rapidly and almost on command. When the sun goes away, it's really hard. We're pretty deep for this time of year, drifting between 35–40 feet. We start to make our way to some shallower water and find a pretty good area in 27 feet that we're sharing with a guide that Larry's friends with. Each drift across this set of rocks

Larry and the author double up on two big smallies!

Anthony Lorefice with two big smallmouth.

takes about twenty minutes, and we're catching about five to eight fish on each drift. We're also losing about four fish on each drift; it's the sloppiest day of fishing I've ever had, and I would have to think that Larry would say the same, especially after I watch him lose a 7-plus-pounder at the boat.

Anthony and I are both drop shotting, but we're cycling through baits like crazy trying to find something that'll produce more fish than the rate we're catching them. When there's no sun the bite dies, and nothing seems to produce more than three or four fish an hour that we're getting. We try a couple other things briefly: a tube, a jig, drop shot. Each of those produce nothing at all.

We make one more move before we call it a day, back to a rocky area where we started and Larry caught that 5.5 pound smallie first thing in the morning. We catch four more there, two of them over 6 pounds, putting our grand total at just under 27 pounds. Not bad at all for a short day (8:30 AM–2:00 PM). I'd get a Facebook message a week later from a guy who had written me a few times in the past saying that he saw me that day. When he described his boat I knew exactly who he was on the water. We had commented on how he was alone when we saw him near where we caught those two 6s and the 5.5. The guy sent a picture to me of a 7.25 he caught after we left. That fish would've pushed our bag to almost 30 pounds, so we were on the right school, we just needed more sun and a little more time.

36

Candlewood

My first time to Candlewood was one of the most memorable fishing trips of my life for many reasons. It was the fall of 2016, and I remember thinking how surprised I was to learn when I put the address in my GPS that it was less than a three-hour drive for me to get to the Squantz launch. For some reason I had always thought that it was farther away, so I chose to fish the waters that were closer to me. When Oneida, Ontario, Cayuga are all close by, it's hard to convince yourself to go on long drives, especially in the fall. Don't get me wrong, I know there are huge fish there. I have great friends in Connecticut and in many

The author and Dave Dziob with a couple of nice smallies to start the day!

ways I think we're in constant competition with each other trying to see who can catch and share bigger fish than the other. Once I started this project it became essential for me to go, and I'm so glad that I did. It's one of those things that just worked out the way that it was meant to.

What do I mean by that? Well, like I said I never had fished this lake before until I went with Dave Dziob. Dave is the owner of Tackle Supply Depot, formerly known as Northern BASS. I met Dave at the Suffern Show in the spring of 2015 (by the way, that's a great show that I encourage any angler to attend), but I didn't really get to know him until we roomed together in a condo down in Orlando, Florida during ICAST in July 2016. That was when we started to talk about this book and when would be the best time for me to go to Candlewood. I was ready to go then, but Dave insisted that we needed to wait as long as possible for reasons that I'll explain later. When I got the text from him in November saying, "It's on right now. Wednesday, Thursday, or Friday. Pick one of them." I jumped at Thursday even though it was going to be a crazy week for me because I knew this would probably be my last opportunity in 2016, but more importantly because I knew if Dave said it was on that we were going to have a chance to do something pretty incredible. So I went to bed at midnight, got up with my youngest son Jason for an hour while he had trouble sleeping, took a 30-minute power nap, and then left my house at 3:30 AM with a whopping one and a half hours of sleep under my belt, and without my #TeamNoSleep partners-in-crime.

This was a solo mission.

Being as tired as I was, I was really glad that it was a short trip. Even the three hours it took me to get there felt fast because it was all highway except for maybe the last twenty minutes before I got to the lake. In that last stretch I noticed two things. The first was that the scenery was really amazing. I had no idea that it would be such a beautiful landscape. The hills are very steep and are littered with giant boulders, and the roads are windy and seem to weave in and out of gullies and narrow passages. When I arrived at the lake it immediately reminded me of the St. Lawrence River. The shorelines and islands are covered with rock faces and steep drop-offs. I was also surprised at how little current there was for a man-made lake of this size. I had expected there to be more, or to learn that the fish responded more like they do in TVA lakes, or at Smith Mountain. Instead it sets up more like the St. Lawrence, where the bluff walls and islands look like great places to find fish, but the underwater structure really is the key.

The difference is that here you're looking for things like old stone walls, foundations of homes and other buildings, or roadways that were cut out for wagons. These are the areas where you find fish here because, once again, this lake was created by building a dam and flooding an area. So you don't really have the traditional rock piles that you do in other areas. You're looking at man-made structures that hold fish. But you also need to know how to approach these areas and the fish that are there. I had heard that Candlewood smallies

Two more big ones for Dave and the author!

were much easier to spook than other fish, and it's true. My friend Jordan said once that he remembered how years ago you could fish for the smallmouth vertically with a drop shot or other finesse presentation but now if you touch the trolling motor the fish will scatter, so you can't stay on a spot. I admit I was a little bit skeptical of that, but he was right, 100 percent. The first time I stepped on the pedal above a school of smallies I watched them disappear. Dave said that was due to extreme amounts of boat pressure on the lake.

And it didn't stop there. The first smallmouth we hooked was mine, and it was only about 12 inches. Just as I released the fish Dave said, "No!" but it was too late and the fish was already in the water. I had caught it on a drop shot in about 25 feet of water and I sent it back down as quick as I could to avoid needing to fizz it, but Dave was really stressed.

"Don't let them go back to the school. They'll educate the other fish now." On the next cast Dave caught a good fish. But once he got it in the boat he let the wind push us away from the spot about 40 yards while he unhooked the fish, and he released it there. He was serious about not releasing the fish where we caught them unless we were going to leave. This was how we handled every fish that we caught that day for the next five hours. It was a constant game of cat and mouse. We'd drive near a spot, but only as close as we absolutely had to. We'd then make the longest casts we could and hope that the wind didn't blow too much slack in the line to keep us from being able to reach our fish. The day was all about precision. You couldn't miss a spot by 4 feet or you wouldn't get bit. For most of the day we targeted old roadbeds and you had to put your bait in that narrow trough that was just a few feet wide, anywhere from 25–50 feet below the surface, and more than 50 feet away in 20 mph winds with gusts over 30 mph.

The other piece of precision that was key for us was our bait choice. We caught one fish on a drop shot then that fish went and told the whole lake and killed it for the rest of the day. The rest of our fish came on blade baits and swimbaits, but very specific colors and presentations of each. The blades had to be perch-colored, had to be casted from a very long distance, and in a specific location. You had to wait for the bait to reach the bottom, then you had to use short, slow lifts, just enough to let the bait flutter three or four times and then let it fall back down. You had to keep your finger on the line the entire time because the bite was very subtle. For the first couple hours we thought we were missing a lot of fish because it felt like they were striking it but not hooking up. We figured out that what they were doing was actually slapping the bait with their side and fins. If you pulled on the bait when they did that they would swim away. But if you left it alone and did nothing, that's when they'd eat it. With the right kind of spinning rod you could tell the difference between the slap and the bite.

Dave with two more big ones to end the day!

The swimbait rig was the same Donkey Kong Rig I explained when I was at Erie with Mazur: a 4- or 5-inch swimbait rigged with an open hook on a football-head jig. Ordinarily Dave would use a ½ oz. football-head jig, but because of the wind we switched to a ¾ oz. This put a much smaller loop in the line when casting across the wind, let us cast a greater distance, and increased the rate of fall to bring our baits to the bottom faster. All this helped to put us in the precise location to put big fish in the boat. When retrieving the bait you had to reel it extremely slow, so that the fish that weren't willing to bite out of hunger would be tempted to do it from a territorial response. Altogether we caught about twenty-five fish in six hours and had three over 5 pounds and two over 6 pounds—a pretty amazing day by anyone's standards, especially for a guy who had never been there before and was running on less than two hours' sleep. I'm already planning my next trip out there. If you wanna go there, make sure you make a run to Tackle Supply Depot to get the 411 on what the fish are doing and what baits you'll need.

37

Lake Ontario

I like to tell the story of my first trip to Lake Erie to anyone who will listen to it. It was roughly three months after my dad passed away, and I hadn't been fishing at all. I really felt like I needed to step away for a little bit. He'd died of cancer in May, and we only found out he was sick five months before that at Christmas. I didn't want to fish, I didn't want to do anything. But I went away for a couple days and stayed at the Mohonk Mountain House in the Catskill Mountains. It's a beautiful resort, located on top of a mountain, beside a glacier lake. I rode horses, taught my girlfriend how to drop shot for smallmouth, and just got over being really sad. And it was there in a little rowboat while teaching her to drop shot that I felt like it was time to go back to the water. So I came home, looked around for any tournament I could enter and found a BFL or something like that out of Henderson Harbor. Believe it or not, I had lived in New York for over thirty years but had never once fished Ontario. No practice, just drove up blind, saw an island on the graph (Galoo) and decided to make the run. The crazy, insane, "Wow, I didn't know the wind was blowing 40 mph out of the west when I was in the harbor" run to the Galoos. The waves were really bad, and I had very little experience in water that big, so it was really challenging for me. Looking back at it, I had no business being out there. It was really dangerous, and I'm very lucky, but I would not advise anyone with as little experience as I had to attempt what I did.

After a long ride with constant motor failure, I finally made it out there. The waves were awful, and I remember at one point being down in the trough and reeling in a fish that was eye-level with me in the wave and seeing my line actually pointing straight out in front of me and I thought to myself, "I wonder if I could just rip that fish directly into the boat from there?" I threw up four or five times. Each time I would immediately feel great for about an hour, and then something would just make me puke again. I caught all my fish on a drop shot fishing vertical (like I always do when I drop shot), with a giant weight and a 6-inch Berkley worm. Every fish went on a beam. When I had a really good limit of fish 4–5 pounds I switched up, like I always do, and put on a white Super Fluke. This bait won't get bit very

My first trip to Chaumont with Captain Bill Lortz, and the author landed his personal best and first fish over 6 pounds.

often, but when it does it's a guarantee that it's a giant. I got the bite, but lost the fish. My friend Sean was close enough to see me lose it. He said, "You lost that fish because you weren't using Trokar hooks, bro. I'm telling you right now you gotta use them! The only bad thing about them is if you hook yourself you ain't pullin' it out, your ass is going to the ER." I can still hear him say that, and it still makes me chuckle. That was the last time I ever fished without a Trokar. And that's the honest-to-God truth about how I first came to use them.

Right after that the lake laid down. I looked in the box and my co-angler agreed that it looked like I had enough to win and he was ready to go, so we decided to head in and not risk further motor problems and not be able to make it back on time. Shortly after I left, Sean hooked a giant, took big fish and first place. I, of course, took second.

Gotta love tournament fishing.

The following week I came back, entered another tournament, this time out of nearby Clayton (St. Lawrence River), made the run *again* and this time I took second place out of 140. Same spot, same baits. Still puking (which I could've done without). But it felt great to be back, to be competing again. It was my birthday in between those events, so I felt like I was distracted in a healthy way. And it started a real hot run for me that lasted about nine months and even had me on the list of Top 500 Anglers in the World. The islands there are incredible. The Galoos, the Ducks, you mention them to anyone from the Northeast and their eyes will light up a little bit because they know how magical they are. Not only does weather keep people away from them, but there is no catch-and-release season here at the Eastern Basin of Lake Ontario, so when you take away that time from December 1 until the third Saturday in June, you're left with about twenty-two to twenty-five weeks of fishing. From which you can easily subtract half for wind and weather. Which means those fish might see bait a hundred times a year. How many do you think they see at Dale Hollow?

Fast forward now to many years later, I've been at Ontario a lot, I'm not getting sick anymore, and I'm finding new places in the harbors. Sodus Bay, Henderson.

Chaumont . . .

I'm telling you right now, there are very few places in the world that can compare to Chaumont Bay. It's basically a lake within a lake, but there's a good reason why it's a world-famous fishery, and why people will travel tens of thousands of miles to go there. With all the recent hype on Mille Lacs and Michigan I definitely think that Chaumont is being overlooked. Part of that is definitely due to the Palaniuk Rule that BASS put on the St. Lawrence River tournaments for the Elite Series, forbidding anglers to run to the lake from Waddington. I completely disagree with this rule, and I think that it hurts the sport, and the

Another giant smallmouth from Chaumont with Captain Lortz!

tournament. If anglers were allowed to make the run to the lake, you'd see huge numbers, and people would be talking about Chaumont like they are those other places. But without a major event there, it's flying under the radar a little bit.

Maybe that's not such a bad thing. My first experience there was with Captain Bill Lortz, of New York Northcountry Bassin'. Bill has been a guide there for a long time and he lives there. He knows that bay as well or better than anyone, and he knew that I was doing some video work and writing, so he offered to take me out if I'd create some content for him. We picked two days when the weather looked good in early July and headed out to find some big ones in the bays. I was excited to see some other parts of the lake that I hadn't explored before. I learned right away that Chaumont is a diverse fishery, with many bays within that bay, and each of them often in different stages of weed growth, water temperature, and clarity. For instance, on the first day we fished with swimbaits in Three Mile and we caught some good numbers, but nothing really big. A couple months later I went back to Three Mile and it was full of green, slimy algae on the bottom, and we caught nothing. That's because this algae is a huge turnoff for smallmouth. If you see this, you can leave. Smallmouth do not like this stuff at all, and will not be there.

We fished some other stuff on that first day and then called it a day. On the second day we fished a different area of Chaumont that we hadn't fished the day before because the wind really didn't allow it. We struggled for almost the entire day, and to be honest, I was starting to get a little cranky because I felt like I was in the smallmouth Mecca, and I couldn't believe

Captain Lortz rounded out our bag with three giants over 5 pounds for an even 27 pounds for the day!

that we weren't smashing them! And then, for twenty-five minutes, we set the world on fire. We found a giant school, and we went almost every single cast, giant after giant after giant. This is where I caught my first 6-pound smallmouth, and where I would eventually catch my first 7-pound smallmouth as well. Both of them came on a swimbait, within 10 feet of each other, three years apart.

This is what makes Chaumont so special: You can go from zero to hero in minutes. I've had this experience here many times. In fact, the more I think about it, I've never drilled them all day at Chaumont. It's been an all-day grind, and then I find a pile of them, and have a livewell of five fish that weigh between 23–30 lbs. The key here is just finding that school. It's knowing certain areas that are not real big, maybe 20–40 yards, and hitting each of them until you find the one that has the school. Sometimes you find the school quicker, but it takes a bit to figure out what they want to eat. But you should never come here without these four baits: tube, fluke, swimbait, and a drop shot. This is a powerfishing dream come true, and you don't bring finesse gear to Chaumont Bay. Ever.

38

Oneida

When people think of going to New York to catch big smallmouth they probably think they have to go to Erie, Ontario, or the St. Lawrence River. Don't get me wrong—those are all tremendous fisheries and I don't fault anyone for wanting to go there. They're beautiful and the water is insanely clear, but let's be honest, you could very easily travel all the way there and find gale-force winds blowing you back to wherever the hell you came from. So at the very least, Oneida is a good backup plan in case that does happen. But what if I told you that it really shouldn't be? That maybe, just maybe, Oneida should be at the top of your list? You'd probably tell me I was crazy. It's not very big, has been widely-known for having much bigger largemouth, and Ontario is less than two hours away. Well, this little gem that runs East and West like a Little O next to the Big O, has some *giant* smallmouth that have exploded in the past two years and are only getting bigger.

Three years ago I was fishing at the east end of Oneida with Palaniuk. Now the east end, for the most part, is a dump. It's all sand, there's no real structure that's conducive to smallmouth once you move beyond Shackleton Shoals (aside from a couple of small points), and it's a long run from the main launch in Brewerton at the other end of the lake. But Brandon wanted to check it out because he had caught some fish there before and didn't really have a reason for why they were there. After a few minutes, he got a bite on a drop shot and pulled in what I had only thought to be rumors at that time: a goby about 5 inches long. This is an adult, fully-grown, near-max-life-expectancy goby. Brandon started jumping up and down, elated. "Do you have any idea how amazing this lake is gonna be in five years?" he asked. "This place sets up *so* well for smallmouth it's gonna be amazing!"

He was so right. Since the invasion of the gobies, Oneida Lake is seeing a tremendous increase in the size of the smallmouth there. What used to be a lake that needed largemouth to win, saw a Bassmaster Open in 2016 that was won entirely on smallmouth (fifteen fish) and all but one of the twelve boats fishing on the final day weighed in five-fish limits of smallmouth every single day. The largemouth factor there has become almost obsolete almost overnight. And this is just the beginning, because people still don't know how big

Brandon Palaniuk and the author (behind the camera) at Oneida Lake.

the smallmouth have gotten and are still (in large part) looking for largemouth there. When the word gets out, it's going to be crazy and I truly believe that many State Record smallmouth will come from this lake over the next several years. Brandon was right about it setting up perfectly for smallmouth. There are countless shoals, there are points, islands, deep channels, and ledges. There are areas with lots of current, and it's just deep enough to have holes the fish can escape to in the summer, but it's shallow enough that the water doesn't get real cold unless we have a terrible winter in New York.

My favorite baits here are a spinnerbait, swimbait, walking bait, and a crankbait. Those four baits are on the front deck all year long. I'll fish them all in deep water, shallow water, and everywhere in between. Generally I start on the shoals in the morning, and then I move to the areas of 8–12 feet in the afternoon during the summer, and deeper areas 15–20 feet deep in the spring and fall. In the spring the fish are shallow and really easy to find. You can beat the banks with swimbaits in the river, or look on the ledges and find them in those very specific areas of 14 feet, 11 feet, or 7 feet of water. In the summer you want to concentrate on transition areas with isolated patches of healthy grass. Don't waste your time on the shoals just yet. Those are smaller fish still, and the biggest fish are still in the 8- to 12-foot zone. Look for those areas that have what I call big brown bowling balls on the bottom. Those are the areas that will hold the giant smallmouth. Now as I write this I'm telling you that I predict that by the summer of 2018 it will be different, more like Mille Lacs, where you'll want to spend your time deeper, and you'll need to learn how to use your electronics to mark fish and target them with vertical presentations.

I've fished many tournaments here, too many to count, but of all of them I'd have to say that my fondest memory is with Destin Demarion. I met Destin when we were both co's at an FLW event at Smith Mountain Lake in Virginia. Years later we decided to fish a small tournament together at Oneida, and I knew days before that it was gonna be an absolute blast. Our styles are very similar, and I really felt like we would catch some big fish that day.

7:00 AM, NOVEMBER

We arrive early to launch like most tournaments do at Oneida, out of Oneida Shores in Brewerton. This launch is located at the west end of the lake (most people who aren't familiar with Oneida make the mistake of thinking it runs north and south, when in fact it runs east and west, with the bridge to Interstate 81 on the farthest western end, marking the entrance to the Oneida River). The plan is to launch and from there we'll run to our favorite areas: Maple Bay, Fisher Bay, Shackleton Shoals, Briggs, South Bay. It's November, so there's no need to try and work fish. We're in full-blown run-and-gun mode. This time of year my eyes are constantly canvassing the lake, looking for any signs of diving birds or busting fish.

We pull up to the ramp and hit the power trip to prepare to launch and nothing happens. Try it again and still nothing. Try the main power on the dash, nothing. Try the trolling motor, and it works. So, the first step is to check the main battery. We use a pair of jumper cables to connect the main battery to the three trolling motor batteries as a test. This is an easy way to see if your main battery is dead rather than going through a long process of unhooking cables. If the jumper cables don't deliver power to the motor you know you have a fuse issue and not a battery issue. When we connect the batteries the power trim down engages (by itself) and won't stop. The only way to stop it is to push the trip up, thereby negating the trim down. If we can't fix this it will be really bad for us. We can't launch the boat if we can't raise the trim. The trim down is running nonstop so we won't be able to leave the power on even while we run the boat or we risk even greater damage to the motor. We start calling everyone we know. We're getting help from the guys at Susquehanna Fishing Tackle, Towne Marine, Brewerton Boatyard, even Palaniuk tries helping us even though it's 4:00 AM his time (thanks buddy!). We finally manage to reset the system just long enough to get the power trim to raise up high enough so we can launch the boat, but that's not a huge victory. We'll be operating under trolling motor only, in 12 mph west winds, with no graphs, no paper maps, no livewells. And we just gave the rest of the field a two-hour head start. Now at this point some would think we were tired and frustrated, that we would just go home. Hell, no.

We're angry. Both of us are fired up. We even make comments out loud about how the rest of the field is going to need that two-hour handicap we gave them, and we head out. But without a real motor, we're limited to only being able to fish the very west of the Lake. We spend about twenty-five minutes trolling out to green buoy to the west so we can drift the main channel from that to the red buoy that is located east about 500 yards. We do this drift about four times, from different tracks, and get nothing. And I mean, not even a chaser or a tap on anything we're throwing. It's about 45°F, we have no idea about the water temp, but I'm guessing it to be around 50°F. It's cloudy, high winds. We should be smashing them on our A-rigs, crankbaits, swimbaits, but instead we're striking out. And nobody around us is catching them, which means they either fished it out, or the fish won't fire. Neither of those are good and only one isn't horrible. But even if we're lucky enough that the fish haven't eaten yet, there's no guarantee that they're even there, because we can't see them on any graph. If we had power and could mark fish we could try different presentations, but that's just not possible. Destin is pretty pissed, and sits down for lunch after a long run to the bridge failed to deliver a fish, which is pretty horrible. If all else fails it's usually safe to say that you can at least catch a few small ones from the I-81 bridge, and sometimes you can catch giants there. Getting a zero there has taken our day from bad to borderline horrible. At this point it's after noon and our only option is to start making our way back to the ramp. At 1:30 PM, not far from where we started the day at 9:30 AM, the sun comes out. And as soon as it does we get our first fish and it's a good one (4-plus). That changes everything. Suddenly we're filling the livewell with a grocery bag and empty water bottle and checking to make sure nobody saw us boat a big one.

Our mood instantly turns again to hell-bent on winning. We're more focused and just had a huge breath of life and hope. Twenty minutes later we get another 4-plus, and things are really looking up. But Destin has caught them both and we're fishing the same bait in the same areas, so I ask him what gear ratio he's using on his A-rig set up and he tells me 7.0:1. That explains it all since we have been reeling at the same turn rate, but mine is a 5.3:1 so it's coming much slower. I speed it up and immediately start catching them. Had I not asked him, I might not have. We have two hours left, and if we can continue to get one 4-pounder every half hour, we'll be right in it at the end with around twenty pounds! We get another

Destin and the author pulling fish out of the livewell at weigh-in.

We salvaged the day because we never gave up. That's the lesson!

one, and another. Putting us at about sixteen pounds, with just one more to go and about forty minutes to get it. Then the sun disappears, and we see that there is nothing but clouds remaining. We manage one small fish on a Ned Rig before the end of the day and come in with about 18.5 pounds.

We had no motor, no electronics, and two hours less than everyone else. But we also had the will to succeed, and to not quit. This is the reality of what it's like to fish at this level. Equipment malfunctions happen, and there are days when you won't get bit until you're almost out of time and sometimes you'll grind out a good finish and sometimes you won't. With everything we had to overcome, I feel like we won.

39

Susquehanna

I'll never forget the moment halfway through my day on the Susquehanna with George Acordi Jr. when I said to him that I was really excited about going to fish a river in West Virginia that I thought was going to be legendary. He looked at me in complete seriousness and said, "Son, you're fishing *the* smallmouth bass river *right now*." The Susquehanna (Sus, Susky) runs through a fairly rural part of Pennsylvania with bits and pieces in New York. Because of the shallow water it's really restricted to just kayaks and canoes or to smallcraft vessels and jetboats, and may not be the place that comes to mind when most people think of

George Acordi Jr. has been fishing this river his entire life and knows it as well or better than anyone.

an incredible smallmouth fishery. So most people pass it on their way to the Great Lakes and never give it any serious consideration when they head out on big smallmouth fishing trips. But that is a colossal mistake. I've known about these wintering holes in the Susquehanna where you can easily catch over a hundred smallmouth in one day and I couldn't wait to fish them with someone who knew the river as well as George.

And who wouldn't be excited? George has fished in the Bassmaster Classic twice, grew up in a family of fishermen that has lived on that river for decades, and is part-owner of one of the most successful tackle shops in the United States. Their big winter event at the shop brings in names like Zona, Ike, Mercer—legends in the sport of fishing. So George could've told me we were going to be fishing with bobbers and gummy bears and I would've tried it. And when he says this is the best smallmouth river in the world, it's worth listening to.

George: This river, more than any other, changes every year.

Me: Really? Why is that?

George: A lot of factors. Temperature, flooding, pollution. I tell everyone that the smallmouth population in rivers like this is like a train, comprised of adult fish. Each car on the train represents a class of fish from a particular year. So this car is from 2005, the next from 2004, then 2003, and so on. And just like the trains you see in passing that have empty cars, there are going to be periods where the fishing is marked by devastating natural disasters. Those horrible floods we had had a tremendous impact on this fishery at the time, but it will also have an impact years later when those classes of fish are empty cars. That's something that we're starting to come into now from those events that took place eight to ten years ago. You're going to see a lack of fish in that 4-pound-plus range for a year or two. The good news is that we can still have days when we catch a hundred fish, and there is a huge group of 3-pounders that are going to bring some of the most incredible fishing anyone has ever seen on this river in four to six years.

And frankly, not only do I believe him, but you have to keep in mind that we're talking about river fish, which, as I have said over and over, are different animals than lake fish. These areas of the Susquehanna river that we're fishing are mainly shallow, and by that, I mean less than 3 feet. So you can't really compare these fish to the fish in the St. Lawrence River. SLR fish have deep pools where they can rest, and there is an abundance of food. The Sus is just not built that way in many areas, and not only is the current stronger, there aren't as many places to hide and the food can be so competitive that you actually find fish positioned in front of the rocks in the current, and not behind.

That's exactly what we found on this trip. And that's when an okay day became incredible. I don't remember if it was George who figured it out first or me, but at about the halfway point in our day we realized that the fish were not behind the rocks like you would normally expect to find them, but in front fighting the current head on. When we figured this out it was like hitting the lottery with our War Eagle Spinnerbaits.

To his point, we were slow-rolling those baits so that they were basically ticking off the bottom the entire time. This was the first time I ever threw that particular spinnerbait, but I can see why it's the best option for that river. George showed me how the head is weighted differently than other spinnerbaits, which allows you to fish it with more versatility than others. This is the key to dissecting a river where presentation is the biggest factor between a great day, and getting skunked. This is also a fishery that's different everywhere you go. I've fished it in New York and near the New York/Pennsylvania border and it's relatively deep, and not at all like the conditions we were fishing here near the Lady Liberty statue.

Some other key points of interest in the Pennsylvania sections of the Sus are Goldsboro and Longlevel. Goldsboro is really different because it has a lot of islands, a lot of really good shorelines with rocks, and it has a nuclear power plant that offers a hot water discharge that can be *loaded* with fish in the right conditions. However, your success at Goldsboro lives and dies with the current. If the water is really low, or the power company isn't pulling a lot of current, you'll struggle because the fish will be scattered all over. When the water flow is where you want it (above 4 but under 5), then the fishing will be fantastic and they'll be easy

The spinnerbait is the bait to use in this river. You can tell everything you need to know about what the fish are doing by how they're eating it and where they are.

This statue is a replica of Lady Liberty that marks one of the most incredible smallmouth fishing areas in the world, "The Statue."

to find because they'll be pinned to the banks. The one thing you need to prepare for and be aware of is the area near and around the nuclear power plant. If you approach the island you will see armed guards with assault rifles (they will appear to be checking locks, but really they're just making their presence known to you). Do not attempt to set foot on that island. Coincidentally, this is also the place where I learned to throw the Donkey Rig, and it's one of the hottest baits to throw here.

The area of note in the Sus is called Longlevel. Longlevel is an area of the Sus that is dammed up to create a giant reservoir. This is one of the few spaces that you can find deep, slow moving water on the lower Susquehanna. It is also the place where I learned to throw a swimbait for smallmouth, which ultimately changed my life. If it weren't for that, I don't know that I would've been able to write this book. That alone flipped a switch in me to take my passion for smallmouth to the most extreme level I could. Longlevel is a tough place for eleven months of the year, but there's a really sweet window in the spring when you can put up some really big numbers of high-quality fish. And if it were ever re-charted to show more accurate nautical charts, it could be incredible in the summer. Until then, stick to April and bring your swimbait.

40

Canadarago

I'm sure at first glance most people are looking at Canadarago saying, "What the heck is that?" Like a lot of lakes in New York, this one happens to have a Native American name. Located just a little bit west of Cooperstown, New York, Canadarago (also spelled "Canda-jarago Lake" or "Caniadaraga Lake") was a lake that I had never fished before because, a) it isn't a high-profile lake with a reputation for big bass in Upstate New York the way that it is for walleye, perch, and crappie; and b) it's the same distance from where I live for me to go to Cayuga, Oneida, and many other places that are really well known. So when my #Team-NoSleep partner Anthony called me and asked me to fish a team tournament there, I didn't even know exactly where it was and needed to look it up. At this point in my life, I'm not really fond of fishing tournaments blind. If I've never been someplace and I don't have time to practice for even a day I won't go unless I'm with someone who has at least some experience there. Since none of that was the case I was leaning towards saying no. But after thinking about it for a little bit I decided it would be a good way to write about how I pick apart a body of water that I've never fished. And what better way to do that than with a buddy and a chance to compete a little bit against some local guys?

We got there about an hour early so we could look over the lake. There was one decent-sized island, and one large, sunken island that is about half the size which apparently was above the lake surface until a really strange flood/wind/ice weather event actually destroyed it and left only the submerged section below the surface. As we drove around we quickly learned that the nautical chart on our Navionics card was about as incorrect as a card could be aside from having the location of the island. The sunken island, for example, read as being 27 feet deep, when in fact most of it is 5–7 feet. I immediately recognized this as being a big problem because were targeting smallmouth, and I needed to know where the transition points were, the humps and bumps and ledges, and I had none of that. Thankfully my Helix 12 units, like a lot of fish finders you can buy today, have some sort of "Chart Live" function that will actually allow you to chart the lake you're fishing in real time. We made several passes through some key areas and found some interesting stuff. I was thankful we'd come an

Sunrise at the ramp.

hour early. If the fish were on the banks we wouldn't end up needing it. If they weren't, and they were out deep, then we'd need every bit of help we could get.

As soon as we launched we (and 90 percent of the field) ran straight across the lake to the island and started fishing there and the two points that submerged at either end. Our baits were pretty standard for fall searching: A-rigs, spinnerbaits, crankbaits. Everyone appeared to be doing the same thing except for the boat drifting behind us, and I noticed that they quickly caught two fish on slower-moving baits they were working on the bottom. I grabbed a jig, and caught a nice smallie on the second cast. We continued to work our way around the island, where there's a deep narrow channel between the island and the eastern shore roughly 150 yards away. We decided to make a run south (into the wind) and drift the steep ledge along the eastern shore. About halfway through our drift Anthony caught a good smallmouth on his bladed A-rig. About twenty minutes later in that same drift he caught another. Shortly after that we grabbed a 2-pound largemouth off the flat on the east shore. What changed since we started was that the sun had finally started to break over the giant mountain on the east shore. At several times that morning I had contemplated running to the west shore to drift some spots there because the sun had been shining on it since much earlier, and there would be a good chance that the fish were more active there. But at the same time I knew that the locals would be pounding the area where we were, and I wanted to keep them off it. It's always a gamble no matter what you do: Stay and guard what you have, or go look for something else and hope you find it. We decided to stay put and it paid off.

About to weigh in, pretty sure we have the win!

Around 1:30 PM we decided to go check out the sunken island, which was a disaster. The island was so poorly marked on the nautical charts that we had no idea where the island ran in relation to the lake, and because the wind was really picking up out of the south it was blowing us into it, so we weren't even able to chart it first and fish it second. Shortly after that I realized that we were on the wrong side when three boats showed up and start drifting the inner edge near the west shore. I didn't want to be boat number four in line, so we strapped everything down and flew back to our spot by the island to finish the day. I got a 3-pounder on a jig with fifteen minutes to go that would put us at around 16 pounds. We needed to get rid of that 2-pound largemouth, but there wasn't enough time and we headed in to the ramp to weigh our fish.

I didn't know any of the people at the ramp except for Matt Ford and his dad. Matt's a good fisherman, and when I saw him on the water (we had been fishing near each other on the backside of the island) he told me he had about seventeen. At the ramp, he said he had a smallie over 5 pounds and a largemouth over 4—tough to beat. He let me peek in his livewell and it seemed he was being a little generous with his weights. Plus his little one was much smaller than ours. I heard everyone complaining about the fishing. Only three boats caught a limit, and some locals were upset they didn't catch a single smallmouth. Without trying to insult anyone I said, "Wait, today was bad?" to which about twelve guys replied that it was (most with four letter words). So I smiled and said, "Then I'm definitely coming back here!" That went over real well.

We were one of the first to weigh in. Our biggest smallmouth, 4.2, was the biggest for most of the weigh-in and third biggest fish of the day behind Matt's 4.42 and the 4.49 largemouth that won big fish. Matt's was his new personal best, so I was really happy for him. We had 16.26 total. I told Matt before he weighed that if I had to lose to anyone I'd want it to be him. He had 16.43. It was a tough loss to take, but a huge victory for us considering we were up against a lot of local studs on a lake we had never fished before. Just goes to show that if you do your research about a species in a particular region, it will translate very easily to different bodies of water.

We found out that we lost by less than a quarter of a pound to the author's buddy and his dad. Not a bad end to the day!

41

Champlain

Sometimes I take a trip and it all works out. Sometimes it all goes to hell. And then there are times like my trip to Champlain in August of 2016 that are some of the most magical moments that I have ever had in my entire life, let alone on the water. To tell you the truth, it's usually a combination of things that makes trips like this so special. The series of events unfold and seem to thwart your every attempt until you have the most amazing twenty minutes that can change everything, just like that. The grinding, and heat, and stress, and fatigue, and hunger, and hurdles vanish in an instant. This trip, this insane, out-of-our-minds run-up-and-back-in-the-same-day excursion, was the best fishing trip of my entire life.

2:00 AM

My alarm goes off. I hit the snooze, but I know I can't do that so I get up. I only just went to bed at midnight, so this was little more than a power nap. I shower, sort my gear, pack my batteries, go down my list:

> Rain gear: Check!
>
> Water: Check!
>
> Drop shot baits: Check!

Then I pause, go back, and grab a bait I haven't thrown in two years, just because something tells me to bring it. Not some huge "I'm the Ghost of Fishing Present" kind of voice, just a little "psst, hey, over here" kinda thing. I have a plan, and this bait isn't part of it, but I grab it anyhow. That bait happens to be a Jackall iShad, in green pumpkin pepper. I've never had a ton of success on it. I've caught a few fish on it before but it's not the first thing I reach for. I also pack some Whip 'Em Baits Disc Worms, Berkley Gulp nightcrawlers in green pumpkin (my favorite bait for drop shotting smallmouth), flukes, swimbaits, tungsten, extra line, hooks, some deep cranks, extra pair of shorts, extra buff, extra hat, extra glove.

I'm only going for a car ride up (four and a half hours), eight hours on the water, and the ride back. I have enough stuff for three days. Clearly I'm a functional zombie.

3:00 AM

My buddy Anthony Lorefice meets me at my house. We pack up and hit the road. Stop for coffee and gas at 3:15, and we're on route 81 N by 3:30, an hour ahead of schedule, so everything looks good. Everything that is, except for our current inability to purchase a fishing license. Because the weather looked terrible, we didn't actually decide to pull the trigger on this trip until the day before (Saturday) at noon. When we started trying to buy our Vermont license online, it kept saying that the site was down. That is still the current status at this point, but we figure we can stop and buy one at a shop there, and they'll at least be able to give us a paper license if nothing else.

5:00 AM

Anthony is driving, and I warn him that if he continues to drive 80-plus mph in a 65-mph zone he'll get a ticket. He says he'll be fine.

5:45 AM

Anthony gets a ticket for 80 in a 65. And spills his bottle of chew spit all over his shorts and cell phone. Double bonus.

6:30 AM

We stop quick at the same rest area we stopped at the last time he and I went to Champlain together for the Bass Pro Shops Northern Open in 2014. First real break of the trip, other than the ticket.

8:15 AM

We meet my buddy Jimmy Kennedy. Not only is Jimmy our guide for the day, but he's a hammer on Champlain and in the Inland Sea in particular. Jimmy is a chef for Cabot, and I met him when we both used to fish FLW. We were staying at the same hotel in northeast Maryland, fishing the Potomac River. He has a daughter about the same age as my son, and we're both from the North, so we chatted a little bit. He told me a story about how his daughter had heart problems as a baby. Not long after that my unborn daughter was diagnosed with Parvo, which impacts her heart and other organs. We were terrified, and freaking out like anyone would, and I remembered Jimmy mentioned a hospital to me, so I asked him about it and told him why.

We've been like brothers ever since.

This is what I love most about this sport. More than anything else, the way that people who fish can and do come together when needed is unlike anything else I've ever seen.

Between Jimmy and myself I'm really certain we can wreck them today. Anthony is a stick too, and having a third rod in the water is a huge bonus! We also agree on three things:

$1 for first fish

$1 for big fish

$1 for little fish

8:30 AM

We decide to hit some New York spots while we wait for the stores to open in Vermont. It's Sunday morning, so none of them are going to open early. The first spot we come to is a submerged point near "The Gut," which is the point where you cross from New York to Vermont. I'm throwing a swimbait, Jimmy is drop shotting, Anthony is throwing a crankbait. We fish this spot for about twenty minutes and run to one similar that's not far away. When we get there, I grab my drop shot and try that. The other guys are switching between different stuff too. Jimmy gets the first fish on a drop shot. It's about 8 inches long. So he's got $1, might even have two by the end of the day (it's pretty small). We manage to catch a couple small fish on crankbaits, but nothing big at all.

8:45 AM

We run to our third spot, about five miles north of The Gut, and have more of the same: two small fish. We spend about forty-five minutes here, and work this point all over. We're marking a lot of fish, but none of them will fire. We decide to start making our way to Vermont and head back to The Gut.

9:00 AM

Just outside the channel into The Gut I catch the first good fish of the day on a drop shot. It's about 2 pounds, and we toss it in the livewell just to get us on the board! I'm pretty sure that

I don't have the "big fish" prize wrapped up, but I talk a little smack to get the guys going. After that we decide it's time to get our licenses and we head to Vermont.

10:00 AM

We pull into a Marina that's got some of the nicest owners you could ever meet. The license system is still down, but at least they're helping us by calling the Conservation Officers. The bad news is that the paper licenses of old aren't even available anymore. Just an added benefit of modern technology. I actually joke to the Conservation Officer that instead of coming out and giving me a ticket, I'll give him the cash for the license, and he can give me that instead. He doesn't share my humor. But there is a store about four miles away that can access the system through some back door, and the owner's daughter offers to drive us. This is really amazing because: a) I'm fishing today, no doubt about that, so I need this license, but also, b) she literally just met us and I can't believe how kind she's being. At that same moment, the website issue is resolved, so we're able to buy online, but I can't thank them enough, and we buy as much stuff from them as we can as a thank-you.

11:30 AM

We are finally fishing in Vermont, under the bridge on the Vermont side of The Gut. We catch a couple here and there. I'm throwing a drop shot, Jimmy's tossing a little jig, and Anthony's switching back and forth between a drop shot and a tube. Even when we're both drop shotting, we're using different baits with different length leaders to try to pin down what they want. Between the three of us there are probably sixty-five different options of colors, styles, sizes, and scents.

12:30 PM

We leave there and run to St. Albans. These are Jimmy's home waters and he shows a series of brush piles he has marked. Many of them are close enough to each other that we can drift from one to the next in a fairly short amount of time thanks to the steady wind that's blowing out of the south-southwest. I'm also incredibly thankful for this wind because without it, it would be brutally hot. Even with the breeze, there's still a blast of humidity that tears through your clothes the second the sun pops out and it's making this day really drag. No good fish yet and we're leaving at 4:00 PM, and that doesn't feel very good to anyone, at all. And I realize that this heat is not the best for large numbers of big smallmouth, but there's a good chance we can find some deep fish, and I'm hopeful.

First good fish of the day!

The brush piles we drift over are loaded with smallies. At times the screen on the graph is almost entirely yellow and red. Lasagna at its finest. This is a clear reminder of why electronics are so important to fishing offshore structure. Without them it is nearly impossible to locate these areas, let alone mark fish on them. These new units are so accurate that we can tell the difference between different types of grasses, we can actually see the trees on the 3-D sonar, and you can tell the smallmouth from the other fish on the 2-D.

We catch a couple here and there but nothing big enough to photograph yet. We drift those four piles six times, trying to get those fish to fire and they just won't. So we decide to make a run and try this spot later.

2:00 PM

We run to a spot that wasn't far from the brush piles, but there's another boat sitting right on the point that we wanted to fish. So we stop and fish farther out, waiting to see if that guy decides to leave. Not long at this spot, Jimmy hooks up on a drop shot with what turns out to be a largemouth that's right around 5 pounds. Not what we were expecting to find in 25 feet, but nobody's complaining. We spend another hour there and we don't catch anything but a couple little fish. At this point, it looks like Jimmy's gonna win two whole United States dollars, and panic is starting to set in a little bit. Jimmy decides to boost morale and take us to one of his best largemouth spots real quick.

2:45 PM

We arrive at the largie spot and on the second cast Anthony hooks up on a drop shot with our second big largemouth of the day, just under 5 pounds at 4.85. Now we have two big fish in the box and the only one without a good one is me. Not wanting to beat that spot up, Jimmy takes us to two other spots not far away that he says hold big smallies. "We won't catch a ton of fish there, but we should catch a couple big ones!" It's a real short drive and we don't even have to pull the trolling motor, just idle over. When we get there we can see again that the spot has a lot of bait and a lot of fish, and the graph is pretty lit up. After a couple minutes, I reach in my bag and grab that package of Jackall iShads I brought with me, put one on, drop down off the side of the boat, and I get bit as soon as the bait hits the water. I reel it in and it's a big largemouth, a little bigger than the one Jimmy caught. Take it off and get it in the box and drop back down and catch a smallmouth that's a little over 4 pounds. Put that fish in the box, drop back down, and get bit again. This time it's a really big largemouth, almost 6 pounds. As Jimmy boats it, he says, "Dude, what are you doing man? This is Lake Champlain!" and I'm so excited all I can do is laugh. I can't even say anything, I just fall to the deck laughing. Jimmy and Anthony are just as surprised as I am. These two fish are in almost 50 feet of water!

But I lost my bait, and I only have two left. I put on another one, drop down, and I hook up with my biggest smallmouth of the year so far. At 6.9 pounds it's not my personal best, but it's still a giant, with a real dark back and the fish is almost black. In less than six minutes

Starting to figure them out!

I just caught three fish that weighed a total of more than seventeen pounds. With Jimmy's and Anthony's best we have a five-fish limit of somewhere around twenty-seven pounds. Granted most of them (four out of five) are green and the wrong color for the purpose of this trip, but that five-fish limit is a giant bag for any lake let alone New York! I lose my last Jackall on the next cast on a huge fish that I lost and never saw. I have no idea what it was.

4:00 PM

We start making our way back to the launch in Plattsburgh. We hit a few spots along the way, find a nice place to release our fish, get some video of them swimming away, and laugh a lot. This picture, where Anthony is holding a smallmouth I caught at the end of the day, shows just how much fun we had. Everyone caught at least one big fish, we caught over fifty fish total, and everyone took home a dollar (Jimmy for first, me for biggest, and Anthony for smallest). On the way in I see this beam of light coming down through the clouds. You can't see the sun, but you can see the rays emitting from behind it, and I reflect on the day. How we made this suicide run up and back in a day with no sleep, got a ticket, struggled to get a license, struggled to catch anything at all, and then set the world on fire for an hour, the last hour. And as corny as it sounds, I realize that this scene with the lake and the clouds, is one of those "Don't Quit" posters you see in the stores. This was one of those days, where our perseverance paid off, and all I could think about when I saw that image was that most people wouldn't have made this trip, wouldn't have worked this hard to get what we got.

Releasing them all healthy to live another day, grow another day.

42

Lake Erie Dragon

Lake Erie is really enormous. It's so big that depending on where you are, you could have nautical conditions that keep you off the water completely, or you could have it slick as glass, all in the same day. On my way out west I stopped in Sandusky, Ohio to fish with Matt Vermilyea, who is a guide there when he's not competing on the Bassmaster Elite Series. Matt knows the area out of Sandusky really well, so we were pretty excited about fishing Peely Island, but in all honesty we were also looking forward to the other areas that weren't so well known. Not only that, but Matt had some secret presentation, and anytime I hear that I'm like a kid on Christmas Eve!

Matt with the first one of the day!

The author's best fish of the day!

So we get there, and the lake is about as calm as you could want from Erie. I've seen it like glass, but that's never a good thing for smallmouth fishing. And asking for wind at Erie is like asking your mother-in-law to come stay with you for a little while. So this 1 foot of chop we have is perfect. We run to our first spot near a power plant and the bottom is loaded with structure that I can see on the graph. What isn't great, is that it's the kind of structure that will gobble up your weights and drop shot rigs. So much so, that I lose fifteen hook-and-sinker combos in seven hours. To put that into perspective for you, I retied my line every five minutes, sometimes faster than that. That was when I put it down, and decided to join Matt and throw his Dragon.

What's the Dragon? Well it's when you take a 1/16 oz. tungsten weight, peg it above a Super Fluke, and drag it on the bottom. You have to make long casts and you have to work the bait pretty quick or it'll get snagged and you'll lose it. The best setup for this presentation is a long spinning rod, with lighter line, 6–8 lb test, and a 4/0 Trokar worm hook. You want to use short, rapid jerking movements with the rod pointed down at the water and pulling to your side. I asked him why he called it the Dragon and he said "Someone asked me how I was fishing it once and I told them I was draggin' it. Sounded like Dragon, so that's what I called it."

Not only did we catch giant smallies, but we caught everything else in that area too—walleye, perch, and my buddy Matty caught the biggest sheepshead I've ever seen on my 6 lb fluorocarbon. It weighed in at 12.5 pounds. We didn't run to Canada while we were there, which is what a lot of people do when they visit that area, because I forgot my passport, didn't have the necessary paperwork with me, and I didn't want to risk an issue even though my Canadian fishing license was up to date and I have traveled there many times. It really is better to be sure that you have all your bases covered before you travel into other waters just to be sure that you don't do something that will prevent you from being able to explore those waters again at a later date.

43

Lake X

_____

When I left Minnesota I drove across the Upper Peninsula, down the Mackinaw Bridge, into Northern Michigan. Prior to that I would have told you the same thing I told everyone else who asked me for the past fifteen years: The Inland Sea is the most beautiful freshwater body of water that I've ever seen. Now I can tell you that not only does the Upper Peninsula blow away the Inland Sea, but I fished eight lakes in just three days that all looked like I was somewhere in the Caribbean (minus the pine trees).

The first day I met Captain Tony DeFilippo near Little Traverse. Tony fished the FLW Tour for years, and was really successful, but was taking some time off to be with his family, so he started guiding. He was referred to me by Greg Mangus, and was eager to take us out as part of the Smallie Tour we were on. I had driven over eleven hours from Mille Lacs that night so that I could meet Tony at 9:00 AM. He took us to one of the smallest lakes I've ever fished for smallmouth. Before we went out I explained to him what I wanted to do and how I typically write articles like this: I give as much info as I can about where I was, what I did, and what I caught. He agreed to that and said it all sounded fine and we headed out. I was really excited because I knew that he had just taken a client here a week ago, and that guy had his best five weigh almost 29 pounds, and they were caught on a single swimbait. Not that I didn't have a great time in Minnesota, because I did, but I love catching big smallies on swimbaits and I was really looking forward to that.

Oddly enough, we started out by targeting the fish in and around a giant sand flat. I lost two fish early, something that I'm not used to. I have found a really good rod, reel, line, and hook combo and I rarely lose fish, so it was concerning to me that I lost two right away. We moved off the sand flat and went to fish on the edge of some reeds. This was really new to me. It resembled Florida fishing, and the water was shallow and crystal clear. The reeds are very tall, and are found (in this lake) in water that is anywhere from 1–5 feet. We started out by targeting the outside edge. The idea is that you either throw your bait into the reeds, and bring it out, or throw it parallel to the weed edge and bring it down the side.

I remember thinking, "Is this guy serious?" when Matty caught a 4-pounder on his first cast, and a 5-pounder on his second. We proceeded to catch them like that, one or two here and there, in and around the reed pockets. We switched gears and went to a windblown point with a steep drop-off. After several casts and drifting both sides without a fish we returned to the reeds and caught about seven more. All of them in that 4- to 5.5-pound range with the exception of one really big one. When we first weighed it, the scale read 6.1 pounds, which would be Matty's new personal best, but it dipped down to 5.5 pounds and was fluctuating a lot. I said when he caught it that it was 6 just by looking at it, and I still believe that it was.

Fishing the reeds is really tough because the fish know how to use them to get away. I lost three fish that wrapped me up in them within seconds of being hooked. The bases of these reeds were really tough and like sandpaper, and you can't just pull through them. This was a big problem for my 7'-3" medium rod and 10 lb fluorocarbon. The only way I could see to reduce the amount of lost fish in the reeds would be to use a much heavier rod and line, which would sacrifice casting distance and hookset capability, and make fighting the fish more difficult due to a reduction in the amount of bend that you could get in the rod for that single

Our best five for the day! We caught some giant fish but it poured on us and we got very few pictures!

hook swimbait. So I was just going to have to accept the fact that I was gonna lose some of them.

All our fish that day came on single swimbaits. We were all throwing big baits, with heavy heads. I was really shocked that we didn't catch any fish on the A-rig. It was really windy, and raining incredibly hard. That's the kind of weather that is textbook for throwing the A-rig and just smashing them on it.

When we got done that day we were totally exhausted. It rained really hard, with driving winds, and I had only slept an hour that night. Our best five weighed just under 26 pounds. I looked at Tony as I shook his hand at the dock and I asked him if that lake gets a lot of pressure. He said that it didn't and asked why I wanted to know. I said, "Ya know all that stuff I said in the beginning about how I'd tell everyone in my story where we were and all that? I don't think I'm gonna tell anyone about this place." Tony laughed, and said I should call it "Lake X." So that's what I'm gonna do. Lake X in Northern Michigan could very well have the next state or world record. It's super small, and you can fish it in any weather, no wind would be too much wind, and you could even fish it with a kayak. If you wanna fish that lake, you'll need to hire Tony as a guide. You can reach him at www.UpNorthSmallmouthCharters.com.

44

Traverse City

Name a place where you can fish a hundred lakes within thirty minutes that are all loaded with giant smallmouth, and are in crystal clear water. Northern Michigan is probably the most beautiful freshwater scenery I've ever witnessed. I had the privilege to fish for two days with Chris Noffsinger, owner of Northern Adventures Fishing. I met Chris at ICAST in Orlando and we set a date in October for two days of bronzeback bull riding. I had never been to northern Michigan, or the Upper Peninsula, but both of them are beautiful, and

First bunch of fish from Day One with Chris Noffsinger.

covered with some of the clearest water I've ever seen. That's coming from a guy who lived on Cayuga for two years and who fishes the St. Lawrence river about thirty times a year. Northern Michigan looks like the Caribbean. The water is blue, green, crystal clear, and the sandbars are breathtaking. Every time we went to a new body of water I thought I'd seen the most beautiful thing there was to see in North America. Their slogan, Pure Michigan, should be the phrase people use when trying to describe a body of water that's absolutely perfect to look at, to touch, to smell, to swim in.

Over the course of the next two days we would fish seven lakes. My favorite of these being the first lake we went to, which I'll refer to as Lake 11. Lake 11 isn't huge, it isn't deep, and it isn't particularly flashy. It has a small single ramp that will hold maybe twenty boats, and it's snuggled between two peaks. We drifted a giant sandbar that was probably four miles long, and saw no less than forty huge smallmouth chasing our baits, trying to take them from the fish we had hooked, and just generally cruising. We drifted it twice, and each drift took about an hour and a half. We could have done that drift twenty times and probably pulled ten fish off every drift, but Chris wanted us to see as much of Northern Michigan as we could, so we were in run-and-gun mode, spending no more than a couple hours at any given spot before moving on to the next honey hole.

That next spot would be the Postage Stamp. It is by far the smallest lake I've ever fished for smallies, and the smallest place on earth I could ever imagine myself reeling in a 5-pounder. On this lake we targeted two humps, fished them both, caught seven fish, snapped some pics, put it back on the rack, and headed to the next lake. But before we left I took a couple minutes to really try to take this place in. Despite it being small in size, it is enormous in beauty. Especially in the fall peak foliage like it was. There was brilliant color in every direction, and despite it being windy it was sunny and the blue sky was really gorgeous.

Next we took a 25-minute drive and went to the clearest lake we would see out of the group. Lake Cari (short for Caribbean for how it looked), was something that I have struggled to describe to people since I saw it. It's deep, long, but the water was the bluest I have ever seen. Even the water in the livewell looked bluer than any other I've ever seen. And when we were launching the boat, there were pieces of giant crawfish on the shore, claws that were longer than my fingers, that were the brightest blue I'd ever seen. Chris said that they eat them there, and that you can even eat the tails like you can lobster. Chris told us he was raised on this lake, and insisted I not mention it by name because he didn't want it overrun by tourists. It's not a place he takes clients normally. We only caught two fish here, but they were both giants and we got them on a drop shot in 25 feet.

One thing I want to stress about this part of Michigan is that every lake is different. Different water temps varying as much as 10 degrees. Different levels of water clarity, and different bottoms and areas (deep ledges, reeds, sandbars, rock piles, shoals, points, etc.) so

Chris with a pig he caught on the Alabama rig.

we wouldn't always do the same thing at each lake or look for fish in the same depths. This is a testament to Chris's knowledge of them all, to be able to know what stage the fish were in at each body of water. It's not easy to predict in the fall, especially on the heels of a massive cold front.

Day two we did more of the same, running from lake to lake, alternating between power fishing and finesse fishing. We threw a lot of A-rigs at the first two lakes. Chris said he toyed with the idea of taking us to Lake 11 again, but Tony (our guide at Lake X) was there and decided that we'd stay away. We did quite a bit of drop shotting at our second stop, Green Lake, where the water was about as green as you can imagine without thinking that it was polluted. Every lake we went to gave up at least one 4-pound fish, and many of them gave up several over 5. Like they said in Minnesota, Chris told us it was waaay off in Traverse City. Which I had kind of expected due to the cold front that dropped the air temp down to 30°F for the first time, and the full moon. I told him that it would be on fire there in less than a week, he agreed, and the pictures he sent in the week following substantiated our speculation. I really think that this is the most amazing place I've ever been in terms of the amount

That *was* the plan, until Oliver caught his first New York smallmouth. After that we would get up every day by 4:00 AM, leave our Cayuga lake house (we were staying at Osprey Manor) and drive two hours one way to Chaumont Bay, ignoring the chance at a double digit largemouth to chase smallies at Ontario.

"Dude, forget those largemouth," said Oliver. "Ontario is insane."

For the record, he's right. But I was a little disappointed to be honest because I had dreams, BIG BASS DREAMS. I understood though, my smallmouth here are unlike many others in the world. Meaner, much more aggressive, and the water is gin clear. Brett Forester (B. C.), Oliver's cameraman who was filming the trip, couldn't believe how much visibility there was and spent every day in the water. Looking back on it now, I'm glad we spent those six days there and not chasing those largemouth at Cayuga. Even with the drive up and back every day, we were catching between twenty-five and fifty fish, none of them under 3.5 pounds with many over 5, and we were able to film some things in the wild that had never been recorded before.

To give you the full backstory before we get to the good stuff, I've got to say that he came at the best time of the year to fish Ontario and the St. Lawrence River. From the opening weekend in June until the second week of July is arguably the best freshwater fishing you will find in the world. The fish are aggressively feeding, they're shallow, and you can powerfish. Drop shots, swimbaits, spinnerbaits and most anything else that's moving can provide you the best shot at a 6-plus-pound fish that you might have all year. And we had other company throughout the week too, which made it that much easier for us to figure them out and find them. Kenichi Ida from Megabass, Elite Series Pro Chris Zaldain and Luke Claussen, my buddy Matty and his twin boys, my son JJ, J. P. Kimbrough, and a young girl named Lauren who I've gotten to know through her parents (owners of Osprey Manor, Wise Owl Landing, Finger Lakes Sausage and Beer, and Finger Lakes Pretzel).

Day 1—7:00 am

First day it's just me, Oliver, and B. C. We launch the boat in Chaumont around 6:00 AM and start one of my favorite drifts. I'm throwing a swimbait, while Oliver and B. C. are throwing drop shots. The wind is pushing us perfectly and we're able to position the boat with minimal assistance from the trolling motor. Many of the fish in the bay have already spawned, and have moved out to deeper water, but there are still some cruisers in here that remain all year. I also know that there are big fish on beds out by the Galoos this time of year, but I want to fish this area while we're here.

Probably fifteen minutes in, B. C., who hasn't started filming yet, catches the first fish of the day, which happens to be his personal best. A phenomenon that will repeat itself later that same day and several more times during their stay with me in New York. He's incredibly excited, and I am reminded why it is that I love teaching people and taking them with me. That look on their face is absolutely perfect. He and Oliver are using spinning gear for their drop shots, something that I used to do a lot when I was younger, but that I don't do much anymore, especially when I'm at Ontario, Erie, or the St. Lawrence because the fish there are too strong and I want to be able to fight back a little bit and not give them the opportunity to jump too many times.

About fifteen minutes later Oliver gets his first fish of the day. Another solid 4-pounder on a drop shot. The magical part of this fight is that the fish dives under the boat and jumps about a foot out of the water on the other side, and we manage to catch it all on video thanks to having GoPro cameras running in multiple locations.

Our drift is about done and we've got two fish in the box in the first half hour. We decide to go up and do the drift again. I get one and we lose one or two and we decide to do the drift again, but a little closer to shore, because we notice that all of our hits are coming within the first five feet of our retrieves. We drift two more times but only get a couple small fish so we leave and go to another spot.

9:30 AM

We have a similar drift that produces one fish and I make the call to run out to the main lake while the wind will allow us to do so (forecasts for double digit winds out of the West/ Southwest are really dangerous and you should use extreme caution in those situations).

10:00 AM

When we arrive at Stoney Island the water is super clear and we can see the fish from quite a long distance. This is where I learn just how much of a cat-and-mouse game it is throwing a drop shot. We're able to see the fish swim at full speed from over 40 yards away but before they hit the bait they stop and swim behind it. This is when we learned that in that moment we had to change it up, and make the bait appear to be fleeing the scene to incite a riot. At that point, the fish go crazy, and would often miss our bait. This is why I said earlier that you can't imagine how many fish you probably miss when you're using a drop shot. We stay here all day. I catch a decent fish on a swimbait, but almost all of our fish will come on the drop shots we're throwing.

4:00 PM

Time to head back. We're really tired, have friends to meet at the house, and will need to get up bright and early to come back up here again tomorrow. Total for the day was well over 20 pounds for our five biggest fish, and we caught roughly thirty smallmouth. B. C. set his Personal Best twice, and Oliver even ran the camera on one of them. At the end of the day it's decided we're spending the rest of the week here.

DAY 2—6:00 AM

Kenichi Ida from Megabass and Chris Zaldain join us first thing in the morning and we immediately make a run back out to the islands to start the day. I'm fishing with Chris; B. C., Oliver, and Kenichi are in the DREAM boat. There's quite a bit more wind today which is making it difficult to see the fish like we could the day before. We do a drift near the ledge of Stoney Island, but come up empty. So we move on to a spot south of the islands that is unmarked by any type of land mass, and without a graph you wouldn't be able to find it. With a straight south wind, we're moving pretty good, and I add a heavier weight to my drop shot to make sure that I can get it down to the bottom where we're fishing (25–30 feet). We catch two quick fish and Chris loses a giant at the boat, but that's all the action we're able to get there.

One giant bag of brown fish!

8:30 AM

We slide off that spot to an underwater point that extends quite a long way out past Calf Island and start working drop shots. B. C. loses a big one, Kenichi catches one, and Oliver gets a pretty good one on a drop shot. We drift that area for an hour or so and move in to Stoney to shoot some video away from the wind. Kenichi and B. C. go with Chris, and I go with Oliver.

10:30 AM

Oliver and I are drop shotting an area that I call "The Bowl" on the backside of Stoney. Oliver feels a tick and starts reeling in his bait, and when he gets it near the boat he can see that it's a goby. This isn't odd; we've caught several on this trip. But as he gets it closer to the boat a giant smallmouth comes up and drills it, nearly ripping the rod out of his hand. This fight is one of the best I have ever seen. Watching that smallmouth eat that goby was one of the most incredible things I've ever seen on the water, and really reminded me of a musky strike. So far this is our biggest fish of the trip, and Oliver is beyond excited. We don't catch any more fish in that area, and with the winds increasing we decide to start making our way back to Chaumont.

And it's a good thing we left when we did. The waves are a lot bigger on our return than they were on our arrival, but they continue to grow and by the time Chris, Kenichi, and B. C. return they're almost nautical. We find a place away from the wind in the bay, power pole down, and snap some pics. It's 3:30 PM and we're all exhausted from battling heavy winds, hot sun, waves, and no sleep for three days.

DAY 3—6:00 AM

Getting up at 4:00 AM and only having three hours of sleep in four days can make you completely dysfunctional. But B. C. helps.

"Dude, you live here, but we don't. As a fisherman, there aren't many places in the world where you can consistently catch smallmouth that are four pounds and up! And as a cameraman, to be able to capture a fish striking underwater you need insanely clear water and fish that are not pressured. This place is incredible."

I get that. But sometimes it's good to be reminded of how lucky I am and that the time that I've invested here hasn't gone unnoticed. It's easy to take it for granted when you see it every day. But to be able to bring people here who don't, and see their faces, is pretty special. Today especially, when I see something I've never seen before.

Oliver with a big smallmouth!

10:00 AM

We move back out to the islands and find a bedded female. B. C. wetsuits up and jumps in with the DSLR and tries to see how close he can get to her. Ironically, she gets very defensive at first, and even charges at him briefly. Can you believe that? This 5-pound fish, trying to chase away a full grown, 180-pound man. Oliver and I laugh, and we can hear B. C. laughing through his snorkeling tube. After a bit she calms down, and almost accepts him being there.

We try a lot of different baits to try to get her to bite, but she won't commit. Bedding smallmouth can be really tough, especially when they can see you, and there are people swimming with a camera in their face for thirty minutes. Finally, after about a half hour and nearly giving up, I take a small tube and pitch it beyond her bed. I drag the tube slowly into it, and stop. We all watch as she comes up, and grabs the bait, and I set the hook. B. C. shoots the whole thing on video, including me jumping up and down on the boat like a kid at the playground while Oliver lands it for me. I can honestly tell you that I've never been so excited to land one fish as I am this one. Not wanting to stress her out more than we already have, we quickly send her to her bed (B. C. delivers her via water taxi). I really can't tell you how special it was to catch that fish. Of all the smallmouth I have ever caught in my life, this one really is in the top 5 most memorable.

Noon

We continue to try to record fish, but none of them are living up to the excitement of the morning until we come across a female that has four males circling around her. The tough part about this is that it's impossible to get it all set up to film. Getting one star to align was hard enough. It's such a delicate thing, when you have wind and needing to position the boat just right so that the sun isn't in the shot, the fish are in the right location, and B. C. is where he needs to be to get the right shot. None of it works out, but we do manage to catch two of the males, one of them is perhaps the longest smallmouth I've seen all year. These fish were very competitive because of the female, so the first chance they had to take out their aggression on something, they took it.

2:00 PM

We return back to Chaumont and work around some of the rock ledges that are near the bluff walls. You'll rarely catch big fish there, but it's really impressive to see and it's loaded with small fish (which can still be a good time when you can catch forty in an hour, and it's

The author, Matty, his two twin boys, and Oliver with a big bag Ontario smallmouth!

a great place to teach someone how to use a drop shot for the first time). We shoot some photos, pack it up, and head in.

DAYS 4 AND 5

For the last two days we focus on the St. Lawrence River, and we're joined by J. P. Kimbrough, who's a collegiate angler from LSU who would later fall just ounces short of competing in his first Bassmaster classic. For being a Southern guy, he's adept with a drop shot. We launch out of Clayton, and begin working our way around the islands. The river is very different this time of year because it has had a constant flow of water with (at times) significant amounts of current, and because of that, the temperature is about 10°F lower than it is out on the lake. This means that the fish are behind, in prespawn mode for the most part, and it makes filming them next to impossible.

Sunset on our final day together in New York!

But this is, in my opinion, the best freshwater fishing you will ever see in your life. This window from opening day until the second week of July is amazing. There are so many fish that have come in the river, and they've been left alone by the lack of a catch-and-release season.

46

Mille Lacs

When I stepped off the water after my third and final day at Mille Lacs and headed to the truck I was laughing at how incredible my three days there had been. Nothing in the world that I had ever experienced in my life would even come close to what I saw and participated in here in Minnesota. Every fish I saw was huge. The walleye, the musky, and the smallmouth. Not only were the smallmouth big, but they were solid, like you could hold them on their sides and they would lay stiff without folding over your hand. Until recently

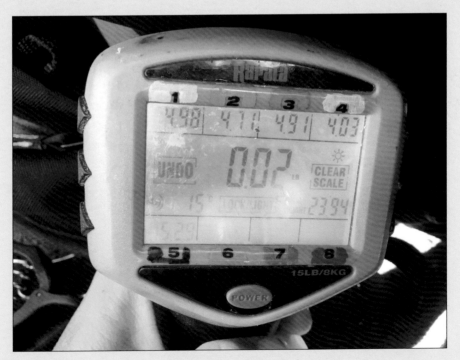

The scale from our first day. We would improve every day after.

very few people had heard about Mille Lacs as a smallmouth fishery. It had been widely regarded as one of the most premiere walleye fisheries in the world, but it suffered a blow to the population that triggered the Minnesota DNR to eliminate all walleye fishing on the lake. With all the industry there that was accustomed to having the capital that the walleye anglers brought, the focus shifted to smallmouth bass, and only then did this lake start to get national recognition. That's why my buddy Matty and I loaded up and drove twenty hours there: to see what we had heard about.

So by now many people have heard of Mille Lacs, but there are many misconceptions. The biggest being that it's a huge lake. It's not a mud puddle, but it's not like one of the Great Lakes. From above it looks like a big circle. When you're in the center of the lake, you can see the shoreline in every direction, even on a foggy day. End-to-end the lake is roughly 22 miles. While there are large amounts of shad, the crayfish are the premiere forage for the fish. On a clear, calm day when you can see the bottom it'll look like it's moving from all the crayfish skirting around. There are several islands, a few points, and a couple of ledges, but what sets this lake apart from any other that I've fished before is the offshore structure. On maps you'll see many different reefs marked. For those of you that aren't familiar with what reefs are, they're the same as shoals or sunken islands; long stretches of underwater structure. On these reefs are some incredible rocks, or should I say boulders, and little-to-no grass. What will set apart your experience here is the type of electronics you have, and your ability to use them. While you can catch fish shallow and around the islands, the best fishing is deep, vertical, and on structure you can only find with the right kind of tools.

My first two days there we had really heavy winds that forced us to fish only the south end of the lake. We hit a couple of islands and reefs (for some reason in Minnesota what we call shoals, they call reefs), one of which held the most amount of fish over the two days. We and our guide Austin Felix would come to call this "The Hammer Hole." Austin is a true genius when it comes to fishing Mille Lacs. His knowledge of that lake and the structure there is incredible, but he's also really great at using his graphs. He's learned the three-step process to locating fish there. The first step is to look for transition areas from the aerial map. The second step is to graph those areas looking for rocks and mark them. The third step is to scan over each of those rocks until you find the ones holding fish.

The first two days our baits were primarily a jig and an A-rig. But it's important to know your local laws, because in Minnesota you're only allowed one hook. So that means that you really don't need a five-wire A-rig. We were using three-wire rigs, with two hitchhikers on the sides, and a hook on the middle wire. This is to help make sure that the rig always swims like it should. We didn't catch a lot of fish either day, but the ones we caught were the right ones and the biggest ones come on the rig. The first two-day totals for our best five were 24-plus and 25-plus. We were told it was slow, and off, because just before we arrived there it got

The author and Austin Felix with some giant Minnesota Gold!

really cold (30°F in the morning), and the lake dropped 10°F. If this is off, I can't imagine what it's like when it's on.

The third day some other friends of mine joined us. Mandy Ulrich was out and took Matty with her, and Minnesota Vikings defensive end Brian Robison was there with his dad and friend Skeeter Fowler. We started south again, but after a couple hours we ran north for the first time and started graphing rock piles. Our second boulder showed a pile of fish that we dropped on with our drop shot rigs and I caught two right away. Every boulder where we marked fish gave up one or two like that, until we found a pile by mistake. Austin broke off a big one, and while he was retying and I was fighting a 4-pounder, we drifted into an area that we hadn't charted. When we were both done and ready to fish again Austin started to move us back, but I caught a small glimpse of red on the screen and told him to stop. That small red area turned into a huge pile of lasagna, and we proceed to catch over fifteen fish from that one spot. At least five times we doubled up. Not one of the fish were under 4 pounds, and

Dialing them in!

most of them were over 5 pounds with two over 6 pounds. Never have I seen such a massive school as this one. And we would have caught more, but we drifted off it and Mandy and Matty decided they'd seen enough of us whacking them and took our spot. Austin and I were drop-shotting different baits. I was using a silver Senko, 3-inch, with silver flakes, and he was using a small Keitech swimbait that he wacky rigged (something I'd never seen before). Both of us had been using relatively short leaders of just 8 inches, which is particularly small considering we were in over 20 feet of water.

What was also interesting was the way the fish wanted the bait presented. When I give instructions and classes on drop shotting I always tell people not to move the bait. However, on this day the fish wouldn't eat it unless you were shaking it like it owed you money. And then, they would hit it so hard that they'd rip the rod out of your hands. I've never had success doing that before, and it still confuses me why this happened to be what triggered these fish. What's also fascinating is the fact that they were so deep. I had a short conversation with Bassmaster Elite Series Pro Matt Heren before I left, and he told me to expect that. He said that I wouldn't be able to catch fish shallow on my swimbait, and that the fish come in shallow in the spring, and stay shallow most of the summer, and once they go deep they stay there until the spring. While we caught a couple fish shallow, the majority of our fish and certainly the biggest of our fish all came deep.

The other bait that is really popular there for smallmouth are shiners that are called "reds." Reds, or redtails, are large shiners, over 3 inches in length. They're very oily, and have a tiny red tint to their tails. Hardcore tournament guys frown upon this bait, but if you're just a guy who loves to fish and wants to catch big smallmouth, this is a great way to do it. Mandy fished them for a little bit so we could see how she did it. She was basically bouncing it off the bottom, dragging it behind the boat. The only downside to using this bait is that they're really expensive and they attract big toothy critters. Giant walleye and musky will gobble up reds and will quickly burn through your stash.

What I also love about Mille Lacs is the culture there: You're surrounded by people who eat, sleep, and breathe fishing. Gas stations sell fishing licenses. Even the small bait shops are full of high-quality gear and knowledgeable staff. Everywhere you go people will recognize you as an angler, male and female, and ask you how you did with enthusiasm and interest. I was asked by my friends there to tell the world how great this place is, so that it'll be protected. I'm telling you as a guy who has fished Erie, Ontario, and The St. Lawrence River hundreds of times, that there is no place on the planet that is a better smallmouth fishery than Mille Lacs. Hopefully I can continue to say that in another ten years.

Jim and Minnesota Vikings Defensive End Brian Robison.

47

The Greatest Smallmouth Fisherman Who Ever Lived

I can't tell all my smallmouth fishing secrets without giving some credit to Greg Mangus. His voice reminds me of my grampa. It's soft but purposeful and he's old school like my grampa was, meaning that he doesn't waste words. On the last leg of my 2016 fall fishing trip from Minnesota, Greg invited me and my buddy Matt to stay with him and his wife, Mary, at their Indiana home, which we accepted gladly. We got in late and went to bed almost immediately. The next day Greg made us breakfast, gave us a tour of his shop, and in between it all shared some pretty incredible stories with us about Kevin Van Dam and his brother Randy, Mark Zona, and his fishing career. Stories that you couldn't hear anywhere else, and that would have you wanting to stay forever.

I'm sure there are a lot of people who are scratching their heads and wondering, "Who is this guy?" I can't tell you in just one chapter why Greg Mangus is the greatest smallmouth fisherman that has ever lived. I don't know if I could tell you that if I wrote an entire book. What I do know is that one of the first things Mark Zona ever said to me was "I would not be where I am today, doing what I'm doing, if it were not for Greg Mangus." That in itself is a pretty powerful testament to the impact that a person has had on another. But Greg's impact goes way beyond just that. Greg has never been the type to keep a secret. Anything he learned, he would share with everyone else, in the hopes that they would take what he told them, and bring back something greater to share in return: A means of building off of

Left to right: the author, Greg Mangus, his wife, and Matty.

Greg giving the author a lesson in how he makes and tunes his crankbaits.

each other, essentially creating the world's first social network for smallmouth anglers. And it worked. Greg's been an influential part of several baits that have become synonymous with smallmouth anglers, but for whatever reason was never credited with having assisted in the design or the research and development. Today his crankbaits, the C-Flash, are handmade in his shop, and retail for $24.99.

Greg was also instrumental in the Lifeline Project in Michigan. This program targets at-risk youth by showing them fishing skills to encourage a positive outlet for them rather than crime and other dangerous behaviors. It's become so successful that the State of Michigan has embraced it fully, recognizing the impact it's had on its juvenile legal system.

"I remember when we would take trips all over the country trying to catch a 5-pound smallie. Now guys like you are travelling all over the world for a 10 or 11. We towed 10-foot johnboats and you guys tow $90,000 rigs. It's a different time entirely but the chase is still the same."

He's right. There I was in his shop, coming off the heels of a 10-day trip that included Erie, Mille Lacs, and seven lakes from Northern Michigan and Traverse City. A total of over four thousand miles, across seven states in just this trip alone, and I left some of the best smallmouth water in the world to do it. I asked him how old he was when he caught his first smallmouth and he said he couldn't remember, but that the first one he can remember was in the early 1970s. He asked me why I was writing a book about smallmouth. I told him that it's not that I don't like largemouth bass fishing, but that anyone can beat the bank with a jig and catch a largemouth, but catching a smallmouth, particularly off shore, is a totally different animal. He cracked this little grin and agreed with me. "You betcha."

I asked him about how he came to know Kevin Van Dam. "His brother Randy and I were tournament partners for years. I had this one technique that I called 'fishing a finesse bait fast,' and I was winning a lot of tournaments doing it, and Kevin said he wanted to learn so we entered a tournament together. I was doing that, and he was doing some of his things he did well and then he said 'Okay, I wanna learn how to do that now,' and I showed him. What you do is you take a long spinning rod, with light line, 6 or 8 lb fluorocarbon, and you make the longest cast you can. Let that bait sink to the bottom, then you make little twitches with it while you reel so it looks like the bait is running away on the bottom. When you do get a bite, you don't want to set the hook real hard, you just wanna kinda reel into it. That was the hardest part for

One of the legendary crankbaits Greg makes.

people to get, to force themselves to resist the urge to set the hook goes against everything you know as a fisherman. But it's the best way to do it and it works."

I asked Greg how they did in the tournament and he smiled. "I think we took sixth, but the funny part is that Kevin is so competitive, most people don't appreciate how much he hates losing. A couple days later I was sitting in Randy's office and Kevin came in. Randy asked him how we did and Kevin said, 'Oh I don't know I think we took third or something'." Hearing that story is eye opening to me because I thought I knew how competitive KVD was, but I didn't. I had no idea that it extended to that level.

Greg and I continued to share stories and thoughts on baits, presentations, and feeding habits. I shared some of my thoughts on swimbaits, something he does a lot also, and what hooks we use and why. We talked about shad, and how their behavior triggers bites from smallmouth. Greg told me something I didn't know that he learned when working with a giant aquarium. "Baitfish want to be together, that's why you see them in those giant balls. The ones that drift off are either wounded or panicking, and those are the first to get eaten." (This has a lot to do with why single swimbaits are so effective). "When the sun is out that ball of baitfish will rise to the surface, and when it sets it will fall to the bottom. That transition from the top to the bottom and back again is when the fish will feed heavily on them during the summer." That I did not know.

We spent less than four hours with Greg in his shop, but I learned a lifetime of information in that time. At one point, we talked about trapshooting and got on the topic of rods and reels. I tell him I'm hoping for an 8'-1/2"-foot rod now that BASS has lifted the 8-foot rod rule. He asked me why, and I explained that I wanted more bend in the rod. He showed that grin again. "You're absolutely right on that," he said. But he disagreed with my belief that the sound of a spinning reel peeling drag is the best noise ever.

"People don't realize how bad that is. Every time that drag is pulling, it's actually tightening. So the amount of drag you had at the start of that cast, or the start of the day for that matter, is increased with each and every pull. You're much better off backreeling. Not only will you eliminate this issue, but you'll also have a lot more control, and you'll pretty much eliminate line twist." I didn't know that, and I can tell you it has taken some time to get accustomed to backreeling, but now that I've started doing it, I can absolutely see the difference in fighting the fish.

Greg also shared a tip with me for those dog days of summer: "When the sun is high and bright and the water is like glass you gotta make them eat. Take a long rod, and a ¾ oz. jig. Make the longest cast you can, and snap the bait up from 6 to 12 and let it fall back to the bottom. Before it hits the bottom you'll probably have the fish on. You need the long rod to make the jig rise as much as possible." He told me this while he put the rings and hooks on a silent crankbait. Then he handed it to me and told me, "That should catch them pretty good when you fish with Mark next week." The Mark he was referring to is Mark Zona, which is a day that I really have Greg to thank for. That, and a million other things that he's done for the fishing industry, and for me.

48

The ZTrain

I will never forget the first time I talked to Mark Zona. I was sitting at my computer writing a piece about Carolina rigging for smallmouth when my cell phone rang with a Michigan number on my caller ID. I answered the phone and said, "Hello?" and heard, "Hey Jim, it's Mark Zona. How are you?" and I felt like a little kid. I also felt like it defined something. That I had achieved a certain level in my smallmouth pursuit. Here's one of the world's most-recognized smallmouth anglers calling me to talk about smallmouth fishing. Simultaneously I also felt incredibly humbled. In that moment I was (and frankly I still am) just a scrawny kid from Oxford, New York who graduated with fifty-five kids in a one-horse town. I felt like I hadn't accomplished enough, committed enough of myself, hadn't given enough to the grind, to deserve that phone call.

Left to right: Matty, the author, Mark Zona, and Ryan McCullough.

I knew I wanted a day with him on the water specifically for this book. I knew I wanted it to be in his hometown, and I knew that I wanted it to be different than the rest. So when we talked about what we would do and how, we settled on the "sub-freezing smallmouth challenge." The rules were simple: Five smallmouth, all keepers (minimum 14 inches), air temperature below freezing at takeoff, and they had to be lakes within less than half an hour from his house. The location stipulation was key,

Mark: "Listen, man, don't think I won't turn this truck around right now and drive to Mille Lacs, cuz I'll do it!"

because that would eliminate the homerun parks like Huron and St. Claire, and actually make it a challenge. When we launched the boat at 7:30 AM on Pearl Harbor Day the air temperature was 28°F, and the water temperature was 35.7°F. Mark had big hopes that we would fish the mouth of a river that fed a small lake near his house and it would deliver at least three of our keepers we needed within thirty minutes, so that we could run to the second lake and get the other two keepers we needed. We were armed with blade baits, small swimbaits (2.5 inches), and little jigs, and I remember thinking, "This can't possibly be as difficult as he's saying it will be."

Famous last words.

The first spot produced zero bites. The shad were nipping the surface and the birds were diving all over them, but the fish were pinned to the bottom and wouldn't eat. And we wouldn't wait. The boat went back on the rack and we headed to the second lake. While we were driving we shared a bunch of stories. Mark told me about a time when he dropped a boat that was less than an hour old off the trailer because the bumpboards were frozen and he didn't latch it before pulling out. We talked about Falcon, Champlain, Cayuga, Oneida. And then we started talking about the Game, the Hustle, and the obsession of smallmouth bass and how it all is intertwined. He talked about how important it is that people not try to cheat the game, and that it will find those people and devour them. We talked about the low points in our careers, and how fishing saved both of our lives. Most importantly, we talked about the responsibility of anglers, particularly the ones who work in the sport, to share this passion, and to teach this craft not just in an improvement sense to someone who's already been fishing, but to someone who hasn't. Mark told me that when he hears someone tell him

"I watched your show and it made me go out and buy a rod and go fishing!" he feels he's done the greatest service to the sport of fishing.

I asked him what's the one thing he would tell someone who asked what he or she has to do to become a pro. Mark said without any hesitation, "T-O-W, man. Time on the Water. Time is critical." And he reiterated that you can't cheat the game; that you need to work harder than anyone else or you won't last a minute. That you have to be willing to fish in December because if you don't, the guy who is will beat your ass because they're hungrier than you are and they want it more than you do. Those are some of the truest words you will ever read as an aspiring smallmouth fisherman. Anyone can grab a jig and pound the bank and catch largemouth. Catching big smallmouth takes time and grind.

We arrived at the second lake and reached a small set of waypoints. Mark said, "We're gonna hit this spot, catch five, then we're gonna go catch a hundred largemouth on swimbaits!" I was down for that, and he caught one on his first cast, but it was a half inch short. My first cast also got bit and it was a big fish, but it shook my lure about thirty seconds into the fight. To say that we were both disappointed by that is a gross understatement. Five minutes later Mark got our first keeper, followed by the second, both on swimbaits. I caught our third on a swimbait, and Mark got the fourth on a blade. Within twenty-five minutes we'd caught five, lost one, and had four keepers. It was only 10:00 AM, so it would seem fairly safe to say that we were going to get our fifth keeper no problem. Except, the two hardest fish to get are always the first and the last.

We struggled for the next three hours. Not to catch fish, because we caught plenty of largemouth, but the smallmouth had vanished on us. This was the risk in the last rule of our challenge. But we wanted it to be interesting, different, not just another "Oh, we caught 147 4-pounders," like we could've done at Huron or St. Claire or Traverse City. We made a run across the lake where we caught a couple small largemouth and Mark said to me, "I'll bet you a dollar I can catch one on the next cast." I said, "Okay." He replied real quick, "I better get it signed, John Hancock!" I laughed and said, "Oh I'll sign it. . ."

Mark Zona holding the dollar the author lost, and subsequently autographed.

Our best four of the day. We caught plenty of fish but failed to get five keepers.

I can't tell you how hard I laughed when I saw him set the hook fifteen seconds into the retrieve on that cast on a 12-inch largemouth. Mark flashed that million-dollar smile and said, "That dollar's going on the mantel when I get home!" Part of me was glad I lost, so I could leave an autograph in Mark Zona's house. I'm actually laughing as I write this because I'm still the scrawny kid; I will always be that kid.

But it was 2:00 PM. We hadn't caught that fifth keeper, and the wind was howling. The water temp had climbed to 42°F, but the wind chill factor was around 20°F, and our guides were freezing up so we decide to call it. No fifth keeper. There would certainly be no 30-pound bag. There would be a story about two guys who loved smallmouth fishing so much that they went out on a day that nobody else was on the water at either lake, and fished in weather that was brutally cold and loved every second of it because they both have the same sickness, and because even though we knew it would be really hard, there was still the possibility (no matter how minute) that we could catch five 7-pounders.

As you can tell, we froze but we still had a real good time.

I keep hearing in my head the thing that Zona said to me that day in the truck about our responsibility to teach people, and the gratification he gets from knowing someone bought a rod because of him. I think about how much he's taught me. How he's always trusted me from the beginning and shared secrets that he doesn't share with people. And I want to tell him that I'm not that guy. That he didn't make me want to buy a rod. But he did make me want to fish the most hallowed smallmouth fisheries in the world, and write a book about it detailing how he changed the game forever.

Acknowledgments

I want to thank the people who have helped make this possible for me. I remember the last time I fished with my dad. I was twelve, and we were in a canoe. He paddled me about as far away from our camp as we could get, to a row of lily pads, and I started chucking a hula popper at the edges of them. I missed countless fish, for what seemed like an eternity, but he stayed there with me and encouraged me to keep trying, so I kept working the same edges until finally one ate my bait. When I had reeled it in it was, at least to me, the biggest fish I had ever seen, and he was so proud of me that he rowed us back to the shore so we could show it to everyone, and he did that with one hand while he kept the fish in the water with the other because I didn't want it to die. We got back to camp, showed everyone, and I let it go. Later that year I got a book from him and my stepmother, with an inscription inside that read, "It takes a special person to catch the biggest fish in North Pond and let it go to swim another day." That moment really was the catalyst for why I was drawn to being on the water every day. If my parents had not taken the time to teach me to appreciate the water and the things in it, I wouldn't be here.

This parental encouragement is why I hold multiple youth fishing expeditions every year. It was also my dad who was largely responsible for my writing this book. He was an incredible writer himself, far better than I in fact. He suggested that I attend college at the State University of New York at Oneonta, where I studied English and creative writing so intensely that I earned a bachelor of science degree. There I had the amazing opportunity to learn from the most wonderful group of professors and fellow students: Dr. Choonoo, Dr. Meanor, Dr. Lee, Dr. Hecht, Steven Rice, and of course Danielle Pieratti who taught the creative writing workshops that I took. I also want to thank peers Shea, Donovan, Quack, Nicole, Guy, and Gramps for pushing me to be better. All of them had so much more raw talent than I did, and our workshops provided endless inspiration. It was such an incredible window of time to be there with them, and I learned so much about writing from that wonderful group of people.

I also want to thank Tim Hine for giving me a chance to write in the fishing industry when nobody else would. Toby Skinner, for taking a chance on me and singlehandedly having more of an impact on my career than anyone else. Brad Lutz, Ryan McCullough, Ryan McCluskey, Nick Lassor, Trish B, The Drake, Barone, Jimmy Kennedy, JRG, Terry Finch for taking four kids fishing in a 12-foot V, my brother Mike for never doubting me and encouraging me to do more, Brandon Palaniuk, Carl and Brian, Jon Fuchs Photography, Shane Durrance, Russ Scalf, and Phil Elgie, my sister, my granny, Pop for teaching me so much about the outdoors, my mom for showing me how to find the strength to get through the hardest days, Matty D, a.k.a Dr. Pattern and The Deacon, Mac and Amy, Kevin and Carol, Potter and Darren, Dan and Lisa, Zona, Mercer, Brian Robison #96, The Weather Channel, Stephen Neslage, Chris VonSeeger, Weather Underground, B.A.S.S., Bill Carson, Jay Cassell for allowing me to write this, The Sim Redmond Band, Lee Rayburn, The Bentz Family (especially Lauren), professor Dave Paul for showing me it was okay to write my own way or else I might not enjoy it as much as I do, and my Cali family. Most importantly I want to thank Mirna, JJ, Sof, and Jason; everything I do is for you.